17th Edition

Aerofilms Guide

FOOTBALL GROUNDS

Fully Revised for the **2009/2010** Season and featuring every
Barclays Premier League and Coca Cola League Club

17th Edition

Aerofilms Guide

FOOTBALL GROUNDS

Fully Revised for the **2009/2010** Season and featuring every
Barclays Premier League and Coca Cola League Club

Ian Allan
PUBLISHING

CONTENTS

Front cover, clockwise from top left:
Cardiff City Ground (Cardiff City), Turf Moor (Burnley);
Elland Road (Leeds United); Sixfields Stadium (Northampton Town).
Back cover: Vicarage Road (Watford).

First published 2009

Reprinted 1993 (twice); Second edition 1994; Third edition 1995; Fourth edition 1996; Fifth edition 1997; Sixth edition 1998; Seventh edition 1999; Eighth edition 2000; Ninth edition 2001; tenth edition 2002; 11th edition 2003, reprinted 2003. 12th edition 2004; 13th edition 2005; 14th edition 2006; 15th edition 2007; 16th edition 2008; 17th edition 2009

ISBN 978 0 7110 3398 6

Published by Ian Allan Publishing

an imprint of Ian Allan Publishing Ltd, Hersham, Surrey KT12 4RG.
Printed by Ian Allan Printing Ltd, Hersham, Surrey KT12 4RG.

Code: 0908/C3

Text © Ian Allan Publishing Ltd 1993-2009
Diagrams © Ian Allan Publishing Ltd 2000-2009
Ground Photography © Corbis
Aerial Photography © Blom Aerofilms 1993-2009

Visit the Ian Allan Publishing web site at www.ianallanpublishing.com

INTRODUCTION

Welcome to the 17th edition of *Aerofilms Guide: Football Grounds*. As with the previous editions, we have endeavoured to update the book to reflect all of the latest changes to Premier and Football League grounds since the publication of the last edition 12 months ago.

For the new season, there is only one fully new ground to record at an existing League club. After several years of trying to relocate from its historic ground at Ninian Park, Cardiff City has finally managed to relocate to its new ground at Leckwith. Of the 92 clubs that comprise the top four divisions in English football, almost one third have now moved grounds over the past 20 years and the pace of relocation seems to be almost accelerating as new grounds are either under construction or proposed for almost a further 10 teams.

Coming up from the Blue Square Premier League are two clubs, only one of which has played host to League football in the past. This is Torquay United, a club that returns to the Football League after an absence of two years. The second team to come up is Burton Albion. Albion moved to its own new ground – the Pirelli Stadium – in 2005 and is, surprisingly, the fourth club from the town to have held a place in the League. Promotion from the top-flight of non-league football for two clubs means relegation for two others and, at the end of the 2008/09 season, Chester and Luton Town both failed to survive, the latter failing to overturn a 30-point deduction imposed for financial problems.

Three teams started the 2008/09 season in negative territory and, during the course of the season, no fewer than three other teams entered Administration with a fourth – Chester – succumbing after the season's close. Of these three, two took a 10-point deduction during the course of the season – costing Darlington a place in the Play-Offs – and the third, Southampton, will start the League One season on minus 10. At the time of writing, progress is being made to ensure that these clubs survive but there remain threats to other clubs as well, with Accrington Stanley, for example, facing a winding-up order over unpaid tax. With the state of the economy, there is a very real threat that, sooner or later, a club will ultimately fold despite the best endeavours of its fans. Given that the Premier League is widely regarded as the wealthiest in the world, never have the disparities between the haves and the have-nots of football been so starkly exposed.

As always the editorial team hopes that you will have an enjoyable season and that your particular team achieves the success that you, as fans, think that it deserves. We trust that, whatever the season ultimately holds for your team, that you will make the most of the opportunities that the season has to offer.

We also hope that you will find this guide of use. As always, please e-mail any comments or corrections to the editor at info@ianallanpublishing.co.uk

Disabled Facilities

We endeavour to list the facilities for disabled spectators at each ground. Readers will appreciate that these facilities can vary in number and quality and that, for most clubs, pre-booking is essential. Some clubs also have dedicated parking for disabled spectators; this again should be pre-booked if available.

Blom Aerofilms Ltd

Blom Aerofilms Limited have been specialists in aerial photography since 1919. Their library of aerial photographs, both new and old, is in excess of 1.5 million images. Aerofilms undertake to commission oblique and vertical survey aerial photography, which is processed and printed in their specialised photographic laboratory. Digital photomaps are prepared using precision scanners.

wembley

Wembley Stadium, Wembley National Stadium Ltd, Empire Way, London HA9 0WS

website: **WWW.WEMBLEYSTADIUM.COM**
tel no: **0844 980 8001**

Fax: 020 8795 5050

Brief History: Inaugurated for the FA Cup Final of 1923, venue for many national and international matches including the World Cup Final of 1966. Also traditionally used for other major sporting events and as a venue for rock concerts and other entertainments. Last used as a football ground for a World Cup qualifier against West Germany in October 2001. The original Wembley with its twin towers was demolished in 2002 when work started on the construction of the new ground. After some delay, the new Wembley was completed in the spring of 2007 with its first major match being the FA Cup Final in May 2007. Record attendance at original Wembley: 126,047; at rebuilt ground: 89,826

(Total) Current Capacity: 90,000 (all-seated)

Visiting Supporters' Allocation: not applicable

Nearest Railway Station: Wembley Complex (Network Rail), Wembley Central (Network Rail and London Underground) and Wembley Park (London Underground)

Parking (Car): Very limited at the ground with residents' only schemes in adjacent housing areas.

Parking (Coach/Bus): As directed

Police Force: Metropolitan

Disabled Visitors' Facilities:

Wheelchairs: 310 spaces for wheelchair-bound fans throughout the ground

Blind: to be confirmed

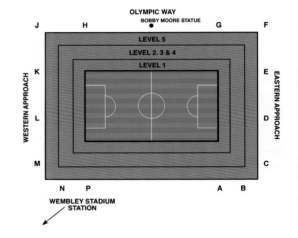

1 Olympic Way
2 Statue of Bobby Moore
3 To Wembley Park station
4 Wembley Complex
  railway station
5 To London Marylebone
6 To Wembley Central
7 Eastern Approach
8 Turnstiles 'G'
9 Turnstiles 'H'
10 Turnstiles 'F'
11 Turnstiles 'E'
12 Turnstiles 'D'

↑ North direction (approx)

◀ 701519
▼ 701513

accrington stanley

Fraser Eagle Stadium, Livingstone Road, Accrington, Lancashire BB5 5BX

website: **WWW.ACCRINGTONSTANLEY.CO.UK**
e:mail: **INFORMATION@ACCRINGTONSTANLEY.CO.UK**
tel no: **0871 4341968**
colours: **WHITE SHIRTS, WHITE SHORTS**
nickname: **THE REDS, STANLEY**
season 2009/10: **LEAGUE TWO**

Last Season: **16th** (p**46**; w**13**; d**11**; l**22**; gf**42**; ga**59**)

Stanley's slow but incremental rise up the League Two table continued in 2008/09 with the club progressing to the dizzy heights of 16th after the 17th achieved the previous year although in terms of the number of points gathered there was a net reduction of one. As with the previous season, Stanley was more pre-occupied with events towards the bottom end of the table, particularly at the start of the campaign when the team managed only two wins and a draw out of the first ten League games, and might conceivably have been relying upon the point deductions at Bournemouth, Luton and Rotherham to survive. Amongst these defeats was a 3-2 reverse at home against promotion chasing Bradford City; nothing odd in that, except Stanley were 2-0 up until the 80th minute. That the team could occasionally compete with the those aiming higher was shown by the home wins against Exeter and Darlington but poor performances against lower teams – such as the two defeats against Chester – were the club's undoing. Although there is some stability in that John Coleman has confirmed that he'll remain manager for 2009/10 there is some uncertainty for the future given that Eric Whalley, who has overseen the development of the club since the mid-1990s, announced in early 2009 that he intended to sell his stake. It looks as though, in 2009/10, that the team will face a greater risk of being drawn into the relegation battle, given that at present no teams will be starting with a points deduction.

Advance Tickets Tel No: 01254 356950
Fax: 01254 356951
Training Ground: King George V Playing Fields, Royds Avenue, Accrington BB5 2JX
Brief History: The original club was formed as Accrington Villa in 1891, becoming Accrington Stanley in 1895. The team entered the Football League in 1921 and remained a member until its resignation in 1962. Following four years outside the League, the original club folded in 1966 and was not resurrected until 1970. The club has been based at the Crown Ground (now called the Fraser Eagle Stadium) since it was reformed but prior to 1966 the original club played at Peel Park, which is now demolished. Record Attendance (at Fraser Eagle Stadium) 4,368
(Total) Current Capacity: 5,057 (2,000 seated)
Visiting Supporters' Allocation: 400-1,500 max (in Whinny Hill Stand – covered)
Nearest Railway Station: Accrington (20min walk)
Parking (Car): Free places at ground located behind both goals; on-street parking in vicinity of ground
Parking (Coach/Bus): As directed
Other Clubs Sharing Ground: Burnley Reserves (tbc)
Police Force and Tel No: Lancashire Police (01254 382141)
Disabled Visitors' Facilities:
Wheelchairs: Available
Blind: No special facility
Anticipated Development(s): In order to meet the deadline of 1 May 2009 to provide the League's requirement of 2,000 covered seats the club has decided to demolish the cover over the Whinney Hill side and replace it with new covered seating accommodation. This was to be allocated to away fans. The Coppice Terrace is also to be extended in order to maintain the ground's 5000 capacity.

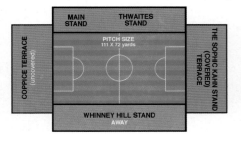

1 A680 Whalley Road
2 To town centre and
  Accrington BR station
  (one mile)
3 Livingstone Road
4 Cleveleys Road
5 Coppice Terrace (away)

↑ North direction (approx)

◀ 701911
▾ 701918

aldershot town

The EBB Stadium at The Recreation Ground, High Street, Aldershot, Hampshire GU11 1TW

website: **WWW.THESHOTS.CO.UK**
e:mail: **ENQUIRIES@THESHOTS.CO.UK**
tel no: **01252 320211**
colours: **RED SHIRTS, RED SHORTS**
nickname: **THE SHOTS**
season 2009/10: **LEAGUE TWO**

Last Season: **15th** (p**46**; w**14**; d**12**; l**20**; gf**59**; ga**80**)

Promoted at the end of the 2007/08 season and thus reclaiming the town's League status after more than a decade, Aldershot had a reasonably secure reintroduction to League football, achieving a creditable position in mid-table. Under Gary Waddock the team produced some good results against the teams expected to do well in the League Two season – with home victories, for example, over Bradford City, Exeter, Gillingham and Wycombe – and losing four games in total in the League at the Recreation Ground. Away from home, however, it was a different story with the team suffering some 16 League defeats. Assuming that the club can maintain its impressive home form and pick up additional points on its travels then in 2009/10 it certainly has the potential to be pushing for a solid top-half position with an outside chance of the Play-Offs.

Advance Tickets Tel No: 01252 320211
Fax: 01252 324347
Training Ground: Address withheld as it's located on MoD property
Brief History: Aldershot FC established in 1926 and played its first game at the Recreation Ground in 1927. Elected to the Football League (Third Division [South]) for the start of the 1932/33 season. Club failed to complete the 1991/92 season and lost its League membership.
A new club, Aldershot Town, was established and, having progressed up the non-league pyramid, won promotion back to the Football League at the end of the 2007/08 season. Record attendance: (as Aldershot) 19,138; (as Aldershot Town) 7,500.
(Total) Current Capacity: 7,100 (1,885 seated)
Visiting Supporters' Allocation: c1,100 (212 seated) in the South Stand and East Bank.
Nearest Railway Station: Aldershot
Parking (Car): Pay & display car parks in the town centre
Parking (Coach/Bus): As directed
Other Clubs Sharing Ground: Reading Reserves
Police Force and Tel No: Hampshire (01962 841534)
Disabled Visitors' Facilities:
Wheelchairs:10 spaces High Street End
Blind: No special facility

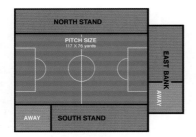

NORTH STAND
PITCH SIZE
117 X 76 yards
EAST BANK
AWAY
AWAY
SOUTH STAND

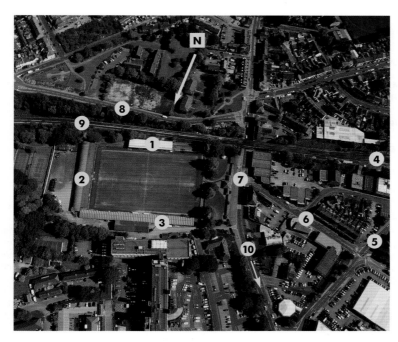

1 South Stand
2 East Bank
3 North Stand
4 Aldershot railway station
5 Windsor Way
6 Victoria Road
7 A323 High Street
8 Redan Road
9 Railway line towards Woking and London
10 A323 towards Fleet

⬆ *North direction (approx)*

◀ 701172
▼ 701171

arsenal

Emirates Stadium, Highbury House, 75 Drayton Park London N5 1BU

website: **WWW.ARSENAL.COM**
e:mail: **CONTACT VIA WEBSITE**
tel no: **020 7619 5003**
colours: **RED AND WHITE SHIRTS, WHITE SHORTS**
nickname: **THE GUNNERS**
season 2009/10: **PREMIER LEAGUE**

Last Season: **4th** (p**38**; w**20**; d**12**; l**6**; gf**68**; ga**37**)

Ultimately, despite the club's involvement in two Cup Semi-Finals, the 2009/10 season was to prove disappointing for Arsene Wenger and his Arsenal team. Although undoubtedly afflicted with injuries to key players – such as Cesc Fabregas and Theo Walcott – a season that had started with considerable promise proved once again to be a considerable disappointment with, towards the end of the campaign, rumblings over Wenger's position amongst both fans and, perhaps more significantly, amongst shareholders. For most teams two Cup Semi-Finals – against Chelsea in the FA Cup and Manchester United in the Champions League (both unfortunately lost) – and fourth place in the League would be considered a success but for Arsenal, starved of silverware since the team won the FA Cup at the end of the 2004/05 season, the failure to bring renewed success was a source of concern, particularly in the way that the Emirates Stadium was no longer the fortress that it had been in previous seasons. For much of the season it looked possible that the Gunners might even not finish in the top four as Aston Villa seemed capable of taking the all-important fourth spot. Wenger's challenge for the new season will be to strengthen an undoubtedly talented – but young – squad, whilst facing the possibility that several senior players such as Emmanuel Adebayor may leave. The signing of Andrey Arshavin in the January transfer window looks astute but Wenger may have to dig deep to bring in additional players. Without significant investment it looks as though the Gunners will again be also-rans in the League and the club's best chance for silverware may well, once again, come through the cup competitions.

Advance Tickets Tel No: 020 7619 5000
Fax: 020 7704 4001
Training Ground: Bell Lane, London Colney, St Albans AL2 1DR
Brief History: Founded 1886 as Royal Arsenal, changed to Woolwich Arsenal in 1891 and Arsenal in 1914. Former grounds: Plumstead Common, Sportsman Ground, Manor Ground (twice), moved to Arsenal Stadium in 1913 and to new Emirates Stadium for start of the 2006/07 season. Record attendance (at Highbury) 73,295; 60,161 (at Emirates Stadium)
(Total) Current Capacity: 60,432
Visiting Supporters' Allocation: 3,000 (South East Corner)
Nearest Railway Station: Finsbury Park or Drayton Park (Network Rail); Arsenal and Holloway Road (Underground)
Parking (Car): Residents' only parking scheme with special permits in the streets surrounding the ground and local road closures on matchdays
Parking (Coach/Bus): Queensland Road and Sobell Centre car park or as directed by the police
Police Force and Tel No: Metropolitan (020 7263 9090)
Disabled Visitors' Facilities:
Wheelchairs: c250 places around the ground
Blind: 98 seats available but over subscribed
Anticipated Development(s): The club moved into the new Emirates Stadium for the start of the 2006/07 season, leaving Highbury, its home for the past 93 years, to be redeveloped as apartments although the work will incorporate the listed structures at the ground.

▲ 700914
◄ 700919

1 North Bridge
2 South Bridge
3 Drayton Park Station
4 Drayton Park
5 East Coast Main Line
6 To Finsbury Park Station
7 To Arsenal
   Underground Station
8 South East Corner (away)

↑ *North direction (approx)*

aston villa

Villa Park, Trinity Road, Birmingham, B6 6HE

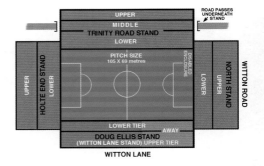

website: **WWW.AVFC.PREMIUMTV.CO.UK**
e:mail: **TICKETSALES@AVFC.CO.UK**
tel no: **0121 327 2299**
colours: **CLARET AND BLUE SHIRTS, WHITE SHORTS**
nickname: **THE VILLANS**
season 2009/10: **PREMIER LEAGUE**

Last Season: **6th** (p**38**; w**17**; d**11**; l**10**; gf**54**; ga **48**)

Ultimately a curate's egg of a season in 2008/09 for Martin O'Neill's team that was to end in partial disappointment. Having retained for a last season the services of Gareth Barry, long a target for Liverpool and now transferred to Manchester City, Villa looked for much of the season as though the team was capable of breaking the 'Big Four's' stranglehold on the Champions League spots. In early February, having defeated Arsenal at the Emirates earlier in the season, Villa stood in third place in the table some eight points ahead of Arsenal (although the Londoners did have a game in hand). This was, however, to be a highpoint in the season as, in the final 13 League matches, Villa could only manage two wins – both 1-0 at home against a Hull City side in freefall down the League table and over relegation-threatened Newcastle United – and five draws. However, the total number of points achieved was sufficient to ensure that European football will again be on offer at Villa Park courtesy of the new Europa League. With several key players – such as Martin Laursen, who's been forced into retirement as a result of injury – likely to depart, the challenge for O'Neill will be to secure players capable of taking Villa higher. The end of the 2008/09 season saw Villa's form that of a team battling against relegation; fans will be hoping that this was just a temporary blip and that the team will once again challenge for a top-four spot. The reality, however, is that a Europa League spot is perhaps the best that the club can aspire to.

Advance Tickets Tel No: 0800 612 0970
Fax: 0121 322 2107
League: F.A. Premier
Training Ground: Bodymoor Heath Lane, Middleton, Tamworth B78 2BB
Brief History: Founded in 1874. Founder Members Football League (1888). Former Grounds: Aston Park and Lower Aston Grounds and Perry Barr, moved to Villa Park (a development of the Lower Aston Grounds) in 1897. Record attendance 76,588
(Total) Current Capacity: 42,640 (all seated)
Visiting Supporters' Allocation: Approx 3,000 in Doug Ellis Stand
Nearest Railway Station: Witton
Parking (Car): Asda car park, Aston Hall Road
Parking (Coach/Bus): Asda car park, Aston Hall Road

(special coach park for visiting supporters situated in Witton Lane)
Police Force and Tel No: West Midlands (0121 322 6010)
Disabled Visitors' Facilities:
Wheelchairs: Trinity Road Stand section
Blind: Commentary by arrangement
Anticipated Development(s): In order to increase the ground's capacity to 51,000 Planning Permission has been obtained to extend the North Stand with two corner in-fills. There is, however, no confirmed timescale for the work to be completed.

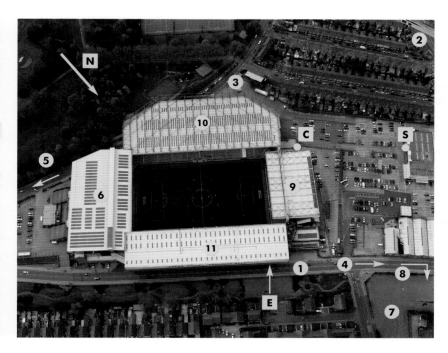

C Club Offices
S Club Shop
E Entrance(s) for visiting
   supporters

1 B4137 Witton Lane
2 B4140 Witton Road
3 Trinity Road
4 To A4040 Aston Lane to A34
   Walsall Road
5 To Aston Expressway & M6
6 Holte End
7 Visitors' Car Park
8 Witton railway station
9 North Stand
10 Trinity Road Stand
11 Doug Ellis Stand

↑ *North direction (approx)*

◄ 701001
▼ 701003

barnet

Underhill Stadium, Barnet Lane, Barnet, Herts EN5 2DN

website: **WWW.BARNETFC.COM**
e:mail: **INFO@BARNETFC.COM**
tel no: **020 8441 6932**
colours: **BLACK/GOLD SHIRTS, BLACK SHORTS**
nickname: **THE BEES**
season 2009/10: **LEAGUE TWO**

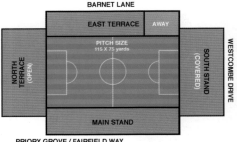

BARNET LANE

EAST TERRACE | AWAY

PITCH SIZE
115 X 75 yards

NORTH TERRACE (OPEN)

SOUTH STAND (COVERED)

WESTCOMBE DRIVE

MAIN STAND

PRIORY GROVE / FAIRFIELD WAY

Last Season: **17th** (p**46**; w**11**; d**15**; l**20**; gf**56**; ga**74**)

After 10 League games and with only seven points achieved – from two wins and a draw – it looked as though the club might only survive in the Football League through the fact that Luton, Bournemouth and Rotherham were below them courtesy of significant points deductions. Amongst the defeats was an embarrassing 5-1 reverse at fellow strugglers Chester City. Following a further poor run of form culminating in a 3-0 defeat at Underhill against Aldershot it was announced that manager Paul Fairclough would stand down as manager following the match against Bournemouth – which Barnet won 2-0 to give the team a cushion of 12 points over the South Coast team – to be replaced by Ian Hendon initially on a caretaker basis. Under Hendon, results – aided by some astute signings during the January transfer window – improved and the club's position in the League improved. With Hendon confirmed as the new permanent boss on a two-year contract, Barnet ultimately finished in 17th position, 11 points above relegated Chester. For 2009/10, however, it's hard to escape the conclusion that the team will again struggle to achieve anything above a mid-table finish.

Advance Tickets Tel No: 020 8449 6325
Fax: 020 8447 0655
Brief History: Founded 1888 as Barnet Alston. Changed name to Barnet (1919). Former grounds: Queens Road and Totteridge Lane; moved to Underhill in 1906. Promoted to Football League 1991; relegated to Conference 2001; promoted to League 2 2005. Record attendance, 11,026
(Total) Current Capacity 5,500
Visiting Supporters' Allocation: 1,000 on South Stand (open) plus 500 on East Terrace is required.
Nearest Railway Station: New Barnet
(High Barnet – Tube)
Parking (Car): Street Parking and High Barnet station
Parking (Coach/Bus): As directed by police
Other Clubs sharing ground: Arsenal Reserves
Police Force and Tel No: Metropolitan (020 8200 2112)
Anticipated Development(s): Following the granting of Planning Permission, the club opened its new £500,000 1,00-seat South Stand on 22 January 2008. The 200 seats from the uncovered temporary stand have been relocated under cover at the northeast side of the ground for use by away fans.

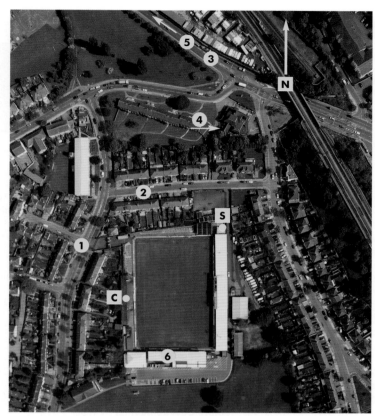

C Club Offices
S Club Shop

1 Barnet Lane
2 Westcombe Drive
3 A1000 Barnet Hill
4 New Barnet BR station (one mile)
5 To High Barnet tube station, M1 and M25
6 Holte End

⬆ *North direction (approx)*

◄ 701191
▼ 701197

barnsley

Oakwell Stadium, Grove Street, Barnsley, S71 1ET

website: **WWW.BARNSLEYFC.CO.UK**
e:mail: **THEREDS@BARNSLEYFC.CO.UK**
tel no: **01226 211211**
colours: **RED SHIRTS, WHITE SHORTS**
nickname: **THE TYKES**
season 2009/10: **CHAMPIONSHIP**

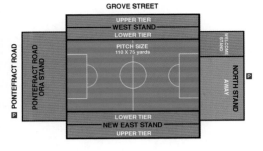

GROVE STREET

UPPER TIER
WEST STAND
LOWER TIER

PITCH SIZE
110 X 75 yards

WELCOME STAND

PONTEFRACT ROAD

PONTEFRACT ROAD ORA STAND

NORTH STAND AWAY

LOWER TIER
NEW EAST STAND
UPPER TIER

Last Season: **20th** (p**46**; w**13**; d**13**; l**20**; gf**45**; ga**58**)

As in 2007/08, Simon Davey's Barnsley team struggled at the wrong end of the League Championship although in 2008/09 there was not even the distraction of a meaningful cup run – indeed from giant killers the Tykes went to giants slain when Crewe of League One defeated the team at Gresty Road in the First Round of the Carling Cup – to provide some light relief. Although never in the drop zone during the course of the season, the club was ultimately sucked into the relegation battle as other teams – most notably Doncaster Rovers – put together a decent set of results. The club's ultimate fate was not determined until the final day of the season. With the third relegation spot to be determined by results at Plymouth, where Barnsley were the visitors, and Charlton, where equally threatened Norwich were to play, the Tykes' 2-1 victory allied to the Canaries' 4-2 defeat resulted in the Norfolk team being relegated. For 2009/10 it looks again as though the Tykes will struggle to retain Championship status.

Advance Tickets Tel No: 0871 226 6777

Fax: 01226 211444

Training Ground: Adjacent to ground

Brief History: Founded in 1887 as Barnsley St Peter's, changed name to Barnsley in 1897. Former Ground: Doncaster Road, Worsboro Bridge until 1888. Record attendance 40,255

(Total) Current Capacity: 23,009 (all seated)

Visiting Supporters' Allocation: 6,000 maximum (all seated; North Stand)

Nearest Railway Station: Barnsley

Parking (Car): Queen's Ground car park

Parking (Coach/Bus): Queen's Ground car park

Police Force and Tel No: South Yorkshire (01266 206161)

Disabled Visitors' Facilities:
Wheelchairs: Purpose built disabled stand
Blind: Commentary available

Future Development(s): With the completion of the new North Stand with its 6,000 capacity, the next phase for the redevelopment of Oakwell will feature the old West Stand with its remaining open seating. There is, however, no timescale for this work.

C Club Offices
S Club Shop
E Entrance(s) for visiting
supporters

1 A628 Pontefract Road
2 To Barnsley Exchange BR
station and M1 Junction 37
(two miles)
3 Queen's Ground Car Park
4 North Stand
5 Grove Street
6 To Town Centre

↑ North direction (approx)

◄ 701015
▼ 701021

birmingham

St Andrew's Stadium, St Andrew's Street, Birmingham B9 4RL

website: **WWW.BCFC.COM**
e:mail: **RECEPTION@BCFC.COM**
tel no: **0844 557 1875**
colours: **BLUE AND WHITE SHIRTS, WHITE SHORTS**
nickname: **THE BLUES**
season 2009/10: **PREMIER LEAGUE**

Last Season: **2nd** (Promoted) (p**46**; w**23**; d**14**; l**9**; gf**54**; ga**37**)

Relegated from the Premier League at the end of the 2007/08 season, Alex McLeish's City made an immediate return to the top flight – although promotion did not come without a struggle and, as with the other teams vying to achieve one of the top two spots, it looked as though City was trying desperately to make life as hard as possible. In the automatic promotion places or the Play-Offs for the entire campaign, it was not until the final games of the season that City's fate was ultimately decided. Three teams – City, Reading and Sheffield United – all had the ability of making the final promotion place with City facing the trickiest task away at Reading's Madejski Stadium. Anything other than a win for City would hand the advantage to the other two teams as both Reading and United had better goal differences although a draw would suffice for City if United failed to win. In the event, Sheffield drew 0-0 at Crystal Palace whilst City's 2-1 victory at Reading brought automatic promotion. As a promoted team, City will have a period of adjustment but the club should also benefit from the fact that it has made an immediate return to the top flight. Although a bottom-half finish is perhaps the best that Blues' fans can look forward to, the club should have the resources to avoid the drop.

Advance Tickets Tel No: 0844 557 1875
Fax: 0844 557 1975
Training Ground: Wast Hall, Redhill Road, Kings Norton, Birmingham B38 9EJ. 0121 244 1401
Brief History: Founded 1875, as Small Heath Alliance. Changed to Small Heath in 1888, Birmingham in 1905, Birmingham City in 1945. Former Grounds: Arthur Street, Ladypool Road, Muntz Street, moved to St Andrew's in 1906. Record attendance 66,844
(Total) Current Capacity: 30,016 (all seated)
Visiting Supporters' Allocation: 3-4,500 in new Railway End (Lower Tier)
Nearest Railway Station: Bordesley
Parking (Car): Street parking
Parking (Coach/Bus): Coventry Road
Police Force and Tel No: West Midlands (0121 772 1169)
Disabled Visitors' Facilities:
Wheelchairs: 90 places; advanced notice required
Blind: Commentary available
Future Development(s): The proposals for the Digbeth ground have not progressed and any future development is likely to involve work at St Andrews, where there are plans for the possible redevelopment of the Main Stand to take the ground's capacity to 36,500. There is no timescale for the £12 million project.

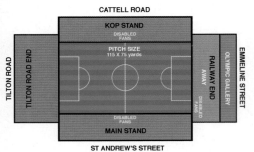

▲ 701032
◀ 701034

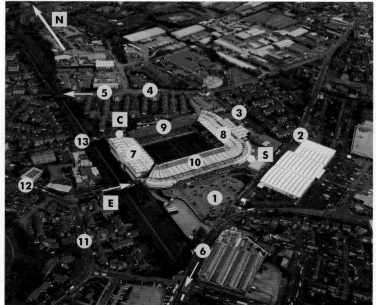

C Club Offices
S Club Shop
E Entrance(s) for visiting
   supporters

1 Car Park
2 B4128 Cattell Road
3 Tilton Road
4 Garrison Lane
5 To A4540 & A38 (M)
6 To City Centre and
   New Street BR Station
   (1½ miles)
7 Railway End
8 Tilton Road End
9 Main Stand
10 Kop Stand
11 Emmeline Street
12 Kingston Road
13 St Andrew's Street

↑ North direction (approx)

21

blackburn rovers

Ewood Park, Blackburn, Lancashire, BB2 4JF

website: **WWW.ROVERS.CO.UK**
e:mail: **COMMERCIAL@ROVERS.CO.UK**
tel no: **0871 702 1875**
colours: **BLUE AND WHITE HALVED SHIRTS, WHITE SHORTS**
nickname: **ROVERS**
season 2009/10: **PREMIER LEAGUE**

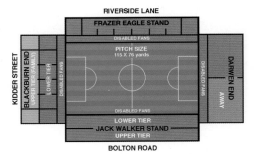

Last Season: **15th** (p**38**; w**10**; d**11**;l**17**; gf**44**; ga**60**)

Starting the season with an untried manager at this level in Paul Ince and having lost players like David Bentley in the close season, the new campaign was always going to be tricky for Rovers and much was to depend on how well the season started. A promising start seemed to bode well with Rovers winning three of their first six League games but a subsequent run of 11 League matches without a win, culminating in a 3-0 reverse at Wigan, left Ince's team in the bottom three, five points adrift of safety, by the middle of December. With a real threat to the club's Premier League status, Ince departed from Ewood Park shortly afterwards to be replaced by the experienced and pragmatic Sam Allardyce. Under the new manager the club's fortunes on the field gradually improved – although the team did suffer the embarrassment of a 1-0 defeat at Championship side Coventry City in an FA Cup Fifth Round replay – and Premier League survival was assured following the 2-0 home victory over fellow strugglers Portsmouth at Ewood Park. Slight concerns for Allardyce must be the fact that his team struggled away from home and the likelihood that further key players, such as Roque Santa Cruz, may well depart in the close season. Allardyce, with Bolton Wanderers, proved that he is capable of keeping teams in the Premier League and, with judicious signings (another of the manager's strengths), Blackburn should be able to face the new season with renewed confidence that a mid-table position at the very least beckons in 2009/10.

Advance Tickets Tel No: 0871 222 1444
Fax: 01254 671042
Training Ground: Brockhall Training Ground, The Avenue, Brockhall Village, Blackburn BB6 8AW
Brief History: Founded 1875. Former Grounds: Oozebooth, Pleasington Cricket Ground, Alexandra Meadows. Moved to Ewood Park in 1890. Founder members of Football League (1888). Record attendance 61,783
(Total) Current Capacity: 31,367
Visiting Supporters' Allocation: 3,914 at the Darwen End
Nearest Railway Station: Blackburn
Parking (Car): Street parking and c800 spaces at ground
Parking (Coach/Bus): As directed by Police
Police Force and Tel No: Lancashire (01254 51212)
Disabled Visitors' Facilities:
Wheelchairs: All sides of the ground
Blind: Commentary available
Anticipated Development(s): There remain plans to redevelop the Riverside (Walker Steel) Stand to take Ewood Park's capacity to c40,000, but there is no confirmation as to if and when this work will be undertaken.

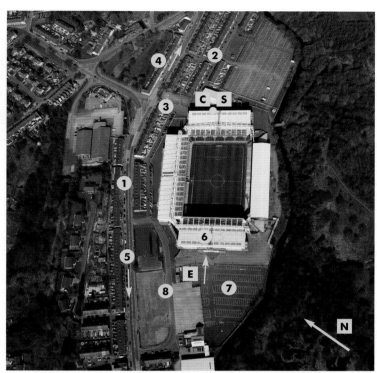

C Club Offices
S Club Shop
E Entrance(s) for visiting
   supporters

1 A666 Bolton Road
2 Kidder Street
3 Nuttall Street
4 Town Centre & Blackburn
  Central BR station
  (1½ miles)
5 To Darwen and Bolton
6 Darwen End
7 Car Parks
8 Top O'Croft Road

↑ North direction (approx)

◀ 701879
▼ 701888

blackpool

Bloomfield Road, Seasiders Way, Blackpool FY1 6JJ

website: **WWW.BLACKPOOLFC.CO.UK**
e:mail: **INFO@BLACKPOOLFC.CO.UK**
tel no: **0871 622 1953**
colours: **TANGERINE SHIRTS, WHITE SHORTS**
nickname: **THE SEASIDERS**
season 2009/10: **CHAMPIONSHIP**

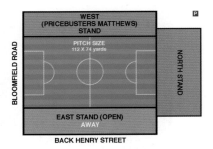

Last Season: **16th** (p**46**; w**13**; d**17**;l**16**; gf **47**; ga**58**)

A difficult third season in the Championship saw fans of the Seasiders fear for their club's survival at this level. Just before Christmas, with the club in a mid-table position, manager Simon Grayson tendered his resignation in order to take over at Leeds United. Grayson, who had been in charge at Bloomfield Road for four years, had guided the club to promotion at the end of the 2006/07 season and had consolidated the club's Championship status over the succeeding two years. Grayson's assistant, Tony Parkes, took charge as caretaker for the remainder of the season. Under his control, it seemed as though the club was initially drifting down the table and faced the possibility of being dragged into the relegation mire. However, two wins and three draws in the final five League matches ensured a mid-table finish – ironically 16th place which is where the club stood when Grayson resigned – with three points more than the total achieved in 2007/08. Away from the League, the club suffered the embarrassment of defeats at Macclesfield (2-0) in the First Round of the Carling Cup and at non-League Torquay (1-0) in the Third Round of the FA Cup. Come the end of the season, Parkes expressed the hope that he'd be offered the full-time position but his wishes were not fulfilled as the ex-Leicester City manager Ian Holloway was appointed to the post. In 2009/10, Blackpool will again probably face a battle to remain at this level and 16th place might again be considered to be a success.

Advance Tickets Tel No: 0871 622 1953

Fax: 01253 405011

Training Ground: Squires Gate Training Ground, Martin Avenue, Lytham St Annes FY8 2SJ

Brief History: Founded 1887, merged with 'South Shore' (1899). Former grounds: Raikes Hall (twice) and Athletic Grounds, Stanley Park, South Shore played at Cow Cap Lane, moved to Bloomfield Road in 1899. Record attendance 38,098

(Total) Current Capacity: 9,731 (all seated)

Visiting Supporters' Allocation: 1,700 (all seated) in East Stand (open)

Nearest Railway Station: Blackpool South

Parking (Car): At Ground and street parking (also behind West Stand – from M55)

Parking (Coach/Bus): Mecca car park (behind North End (also behind West Stand – from M55)

Other Club Sharing Ground: Blackpool Panthers RLFC

Police Force and Tel No: Lancashire (01253 293933)

Disabled Visitors' Facilities:

Wheelchairs: North and West stands

Blind: Commentary available (limited numbers)

Anticipated Development(s): Work has now started on the construction of the new 3,500-seast South Stand. Once completed it is understood that it will be allocated to home fans with away supporters transferred from the open East Stand to the North Stand. Once completed – scheduled for the 2009/10 season – the ground's capacity will be increased to c13,500.

1 Car Park
2 To Blackpool South BR
   Station (1½ miles) and
   M55 Junction 4
3 Bloomfield Road
4 A5099 Central Drive
5 Henry Street
6 East Stand (away)
7 Site of South Stand
8 West (Pricebusters Matthews)
   Stand
9 North Stand

↑ *North direction (approx)*

◄ 702017
▼ 702020

bolton wanderers

Reebok Stadium, Burnden Way, Lostock, Bolton BL:6 6JW

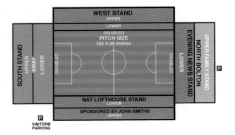

website: **WWW.BWFC.CO.UK**
e:mail: **RECEPTION@BWFC.CO.UK**
tel no: **0844 871 2932**
colours: **WHITE SHIRTS, WHITE SHORTS**
nickname: **THE TROTTERS**
season 2009/10: **PREMIER LEAGUE**

Last Season: **13th (p38; w11; d8; l19; gf41; ga53)**

Although not universally popular, Gary Megson has, like one of his predecessors at the Reebok Stadium, Sam Allardyce, proved himself capable of pragmatism in managing a relatively unfashionable team like Bolton Wanderers into a team that can grind out results and ensure a sufficient number of points, come the end of the season, to gain Premier League survival. A poor start to the campaign, with two wins and two draws in the club's first 10 League fixtures compounded by a 2-1 defeat away at League One Northampton Town in the Second Round of the Carling Cup, saw the team in the drop zone and the pressure mount on Megson. The next 17 League matches then produced eight wins and a draw to take the team to a position of mid-table safety by the beginning of March. However, the team then suffered a late loss of form, winning only one of the last 11 matches with four of the last five matches being drawn. Bolton are the perpetual battlers to stay in the Premier League; the team's doggedness should ensure that, once again, the team survives come the end of the 2009/10 campaign but it could be a close-run thing.

Advance Tickets Tel No: 0844 871 2932
Fax: 01204 673 773
Training Ground: Euxton Training Ground, Euxton Lane, Chorley PR7 6FA
Brief History: Founded 1874 as Christ Church; name changed 1877. Former grounds: Several Fields, Pikes Lane (1880-95) and Burnden Park (1895-1997). Moved to Reebok Stadium for 1997/98 season. Record attendance (Burnden Park): 69,912. Record attendance of 28,353 at Reebok Stadium
(Total) Current Capacity: 28,723 (all seated)
Visiting Supporters' Allocation: 5,000 maximum (South Stand)
Nearest Railway Station: Horwich Parkway
Parking (Car): 2,800 places at ground with up to 3,000 others in proximity
Parking (Coach/Bus): As directed
Police Force and Tel No: Greater Manchester (01204 522466)
Disabled Visitors' Facilities:
Wheelchairs: c100 places around the ground
Blind: Commentary available
Anticipated Developments(s): The station at Horwich Parkway has now opened. There are currently no further plans for the development of the Reebok Stadium.

1. To Junction 6 of M61
2. A6027 Horwich link road
3. South Stand (away)
4. North Stand
5. Nat Lofthouse Stand
6. West Stand
7. M61 northbound to M6 and Preston (at J6)
8. M61 southbound to Manchester (at J6)
9. To Horwich and Bolton
10. To Lostock Junction BR station
11. To Horwich Parkway station

↑ *North direction (approx)*

◄ 700989
▼ 700996

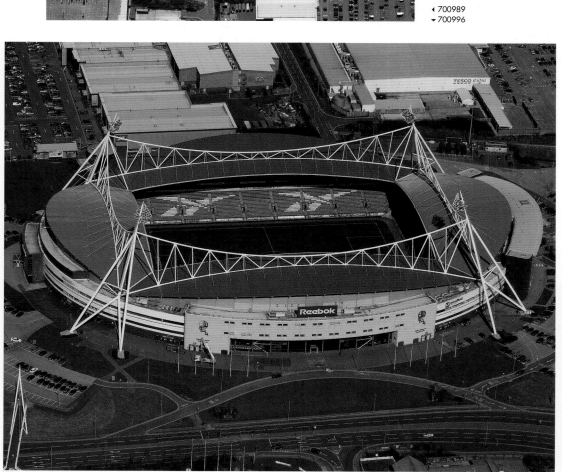

bournemouth

Dean Court, Kings Park, Bournemouth, Dorset, BH7 7AF

website: **WWW.AFCB.CO.UK**
e:mail: **ENQUIRIES@AFCB.CO.UK**
tel no: **01202 726300**
colours: **RED AND BLACK SHIRTS, BLACK SHORTS**
nickname: **THE CHERRIES**
season 2009/10: **LEAGUE TWO**

Last Season*: **21st** (p**46**; w**17**; d**12**; l**17**; gf**59**; ga**51**;)

The first managerial casualty of the new season occurred in early September when, after some 22 months in the job, Kevin Bond was sacked at Bournemouth. Facing a 17-point deduction at the start of the campaign, two points from the club's first four League games following relegation at the end of the 2007/08 campaign sealed Bond's fate. The club moved quickly to appoint ex-player Jimmy Quinn, most recent the manager at Cambridge United, to the job. However, Quinn was not to remain in the post for long, departing from Dean Court following the 2-0 home defeat to fellow strugglers Barnet, a result that left the team still in the bottom two and still seven points adrift of 22nd place and Grimsby Town. Eddie Howe, previously one of Kevin Bond's management team, was brought in to replace him. Howe, at 31 the youngest manager in the Football League, guided Bournemouth towards the great escape; although League survival was not secured until the final home game of the season when the team defeated relegation-threatened Grimsby Town. Finishing 21st, given the point deduction, was a considerable triumph; without that penalty, the team would have finished comfortably in the top half of the table and this will give fans hope that 2009/10 will see the team more involved in events at the top rather than the bottom of the table. The only fly in the ointment is the ongoing uncertainty about the club's future ownership; unless this is speedily resolved it cannot but harm Howe's chances of strengthening the squad for the new season.

Advance Tickets Tel No: 01202 726338
Fax: 01202 726373
Training Ground: Canford School, Court House, Canford Magna, Wimborne BH21 3AF
Brief History: Founded 1890 as Boscombe St. John's, changed to Boscombe (1899), Bournemouth & Boscombe Athletic (1923) and A.F.C. Bournemouth (1971). Former grounds Kings Park (twice) and Castlemain Road, Pokesdown. Moved to Dean Court in 1910. Record attendance 28,799; since rebuilding: 10,375
(Total) Current Capacity: 10,700 (all seated)
Visiting Supporters' Allocation: 1,500 in East Stand (can be increased to 2,000 if required)
Nearest Railway Station: Bournemouth
Parking (Car): Large car park adjacent ground
Parking (Coach/Bus): Large car park adjacent ground
Police Force and Tel No: Dorset (01202 552099)
Disabled Visitors' Facilities:
Wheelchairs: 100 spaces
Blind: No special facility
Anticipated Development(s): The club still intends to construct a South Stand at Dean Court, taking the ground's capacity to just under 12,000 but there is no confirmed schedule.

17 points deducted as a result of going into Administration in 2008

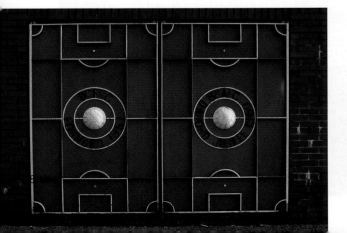

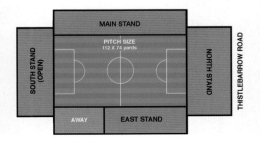

C Club Offices

1 Car Park
2 A338 Wessex Way
3 To Bournemouth BR Station (1½ miles)
4 To A31 & M27
5 Thistlebarrow Road
6 King's Park Drive
7 Littledown Avenue
8 North Stand
9 Main Stand
10 East Stand
11 Site of proposed South Stand

⬆ *North direction (approx)*

◄ 701244
▼ 701253

bradford city

Coral Windows Stadium, Valley Parade, Bradford, BD8 7DY

website: **WWW.BRADFORDCITYFC.CO.UK**
e:mail: **BRADFORDCITYFC@COMPUSERVE.COM**
tel no: **01274 773355**
colours: **CLARET AND AMBER SHIRTS, CLARET SHORTS**
nickname: **THE BANTAMS**
season 2009/10: **LEAGUE TWO**

Last Season: **9th** (p**46**; w**18**; d**13**; l**15**; gf**66**; ga**55**)

Widely seen as one of the pre-season favourites for automatic promotion, Stuart McCall's Bradford City had one of the biggest budgets amongst all League Two teams and, for much of the season, it appeared that the Bantams would certainly make the Play-Offs at least. However, a late loss of form, which saw the team win only two of the last 11 games, meant that the club just missed out on the Play-Offs. Towards the end of the season, McCall's position came into question as he suggested himself that he'd stand down if the club failed to make the Play-Offs and certain fans also started to question his ability to guide the team back to League One. In the event, McCall decided to remain although the club's budget for 2009/10 has been much reduced. Given the straitened circumstances that many lower league clubs will find themselves in, City's position is likely to be no worse than a number of others. Provided that McCall can retain the core of the 2008/09 squad and recruit sensibly for the new campaign, City, with its enormous fan base, ought once again to be challenging for the Play-Offs at the very least.

Advance Tickets Tel No: 01274 770012
Fax: 01274 773356
Training Ground: Rawdon Meadows, Apperley Bridge, Bradford
Brief History: Founded 1903 (formerly Manningham Northern Union Rugby Club founded in 1876). Continued use of Valley Parade, joined 2nd Division on re-formation. Record attendance: 39,146
(Total) Current Capacity: 25,136 (All seated)
Visiting Supporters' Allocation: 1,300-1,800 (all seated) in Midland Stand
Nearest Railway Station: Bradford Forster Square
Parking (Car): Street parking and car parks
Parking (Coach/Bus): As directed by Police
Police Force and Tel No: West Yorkshire (01274 723422)
Disabled Visitors' Facilities:
Wheelchairs: 110 places in Sunwin, CIBA and Carlsberg stands
Blind: Commentary available
Anticipated Development(s): With work on the Main (Sunwin) Stand now completed, Valley Parade has a slightly imbalanced look. The club has proposals for the reconstruction of the Midland Road (Yorkshire First) Stand to take the ground's capacity to 30,000, although, given the club's current League position, there is no time-scale.

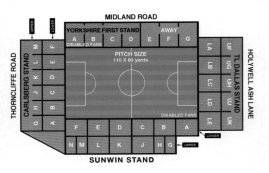

C Club Offices
S Club Shop
E Entrance(s) for visiting
supporters

1 Midland Road
2 Valley Parade
3 A650 Manningham Lane
4 To City Centre, Forster
Square and Interchange BR
Stations M606 & M62
5 To Keighley
6 Car Parks
7 Sunwin Stand
8 Midland (Yorkshire First)
Stand
9 TL Dallas Stand
10 Carlsberg Stand

⬆ North direction (approx)

◀ 701968
▼ 701086

brentford

Griffin Park, Braemar Road, Brentford, Middlesex, TW8 0NT

website: **WWW.BRENTFORDFC.CO.UK**
e:mail: **ENQUIRIES@BRENTFORDFC.CO.UK**
tel no: **0845 3456 442**
colours: **RED AND WHITE STRIPES, BLACK SHORTS**
nickname: **THE BEES**
season 2009/10: **LEAGUE ONE**

Last Season: **1st** (promoted) (p**46**; w**23**; d**16**; l**7**; gf**65**; ga**36**)

Under Andy Scott, appointed to replace Terry Butcher in late 2007, Brentford continued the impressive form that had seen them march up the League Two table during the second half of the 2007/08 season and, right from the start of the 2008/09 campaign – with only one defeat in the first 15 League matches – the club was in the hunt for automatic promotion. In a tight division, with a number of clubs forming a breakaway group chasing automatic promotion and the Play-Off places, no one team dominated League Two as MK Dons and Peterborough had done the previous year and it often appeared that teams seemed unable to mount a sustained push for prolonged periods as the top-ten teams constantly swapped places and took points off each other. Eventually, however, Brentford came out from the pack and were in the automatic promotion places for the bulk of the season. Promotion and the League Two title were both confirmed following a 3-1 victory away at Darlington. As a promoted team, it may take Brentford some time to settle in League One, but the team could well be a surprise package at the higher level and threaten more established teams for a Play-Off place.

Advance Tickets Tel No: 0845 3456 442
Fax: 020 8568 9940
Training Ground: Osterley Training Ground, 100 Jersey Road, Hounslow TW5 0TP
Brief History: Founded 1889. Former Grounds: Clifden House Ground, Benn's Field (Little Ealing), Shotters Field, Cross Roads, Boston Park Cricket Ground, moved to Griffin Park in 1904. Founder-members Third Division (1920). Record attendance 38,678
(Total) Current Capacity: 12,763 (8,905 seated)
Visiting Supporters' Allocation: 1,600 in Brook Road Stand (600 seated)
Nearest Railway Station: Brentford, South Ealing (tube)
Parking (Car): Street parking (restricted)
Parking (Coach/Bus): Layton Road car park
Other Club Sharing Ground: Chelsea Reserves
Police Force and Tel No: Metropolitan (020 8577 1212)
Disabled Visitors' Facilities:
Wheelchairs: Braemar Road
Blind: Commentary available
Anticipated Development(s): Although the club still intends to relocate, a roof was installed over the Ealing Road Terrace in 2007 with home fans being transferred to that end. With a view to relocation, a site on Lionel Road has been identified although there is no confirmed timetable as to when or if work will commence.

C Club Offices
S Club Shop
E Entrance(s) for visiting
  supporters

1 Ealing Road
2 Braemar Road
3 Brook Road South
4 To M4 (1/4 mile) & South
  Ealing Tube Station
  (1 mile)
5 Brentford BR Station
6 To A315 High Street
  & Kew Bridge
7 New Road
8 Ealing Road Terrace
9 Brook Road Stand (away)

↑ North direction (approx)

◄ 701308
▼ 701306

brighton and hove albion

Withdean Stadium, Tongdean Lane, Brighton, BN1 5JD

website: **WWW.SEAGULLS.CO.UK**
e:mail: **SEAGULLS@BHAFC.CO.UK**
tel no: **01273 695400**
colours: **BLUE AND WHITE STRIPED SHIRTS, WHITE SHORTS**
nickname: **THE SEAGULLS**
season 2009/10: **LEAGUE ONE**

Last Season: **16th** (p**46**; w**13**; d**13**; l**20**; gf**55**; ga**70**)

Micky Adams' return to the Seagulls – he was reappointed to the managerial role towards the end of the 2007/08 season – was destined to be relatively short-lived as he departed from the club after the 2-0 home defeat by Carlisle United, a result that left the team in the relegation zone. Following his departure, the club ultimately appointed Russell Slade in March 2009; under Slade the Seagulls retained their League One status – just – although it was not guaranteed until the final game of the season. The final Saturday of the campaign saw five teams – Crewe, Carlisle, Brighton, Northampton and Hartlepool – all with a mathematical chance of relegation, although Crewe's dismal goal difference had already effectively consigned them to the drop. As a result it was one from four with the Seagulls at home to Stockport County. A 1-0 home victory saw the team rise to the dizzy heights of 16th. Away from the League, the team achieved a notable victory at home in the Third Round of the Carling Cup when the Seagulls defeated Manchester City on penalties following a 1-1 draw after extra time. For the new season, Slade's experience at this level of football should ensure a mid-table position at the very least.

Advance Ticket Tel No: 01273 776992
Fax: 01273 648179
Training Ground: University of Sussex, Falmer Sports Complex, Ridge Road, Falmer, Brighton BN1 9PL
Brief History: Founded 1900 as Brighton & Hove Rangers, changed to Brighton & Hove Albion 1902. Former grounds: Home Farm (Withdean), County Ground, Goldstone Ground (1902-1997), Priestfield Stadium (ground share with Gillingham) 1997-1999; moved to Withdean Stadium 1999. Founder members of the 3rd Division 1920. Record attendance (at Goldstone Ground): 36,747; at Withdean Stadium: 8,691.
(Total) Current Capacity: 8,850 (all seated)
Visiting Supporters' Allocation: 900 max on open West Stand
Nearest Railway Station: Preston Park
Parking (Cars): Street parking in the immediate vicinity of the ground is residents' only. This will be strictly enforced and it is suggested that intending visitors should use parking facilities away from the ground and use the proposed park and ride bus services that will be provided.
Parking (Coach/Bus): As directed
Police Force and Tel No: Sussex (01273 778922)
Disabled Visitors' Facilities
Wheelchairs: Facilities in both North and South stands
Blind: No special facility
Anticipated Development(s): After years of frustration, work finally commenced on the new 22,500-seat Falmer stadium in December 2008. Until the new ground is completed, Albion had been granted permission to continue playing at the Withdean Stadium until 2011. Preliminary work on the construction of the ground – the widening of Village Way – started in December 2008 and actual construction – following some minor adjustments to the planning consent granted in February 2009 – commenced in April 2009.

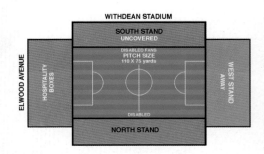

34

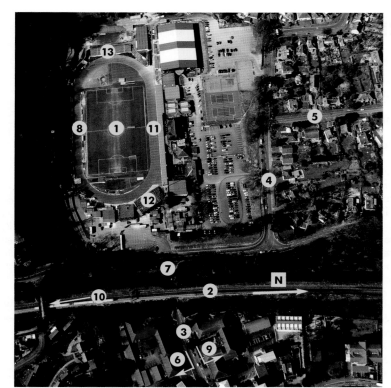

Shop Address:
6 Queen's Road, Brighton
Note: All games at Withdean will be
      all-ticket with no cash
      admissions on the day.

1 Withdean Stadium
2 London-Brighton railway line
3 To London Road (A23)
4 Tongdean Lane
5 Valley Drive
6 To Brighton town centre
   and main railway station
   (1.75 miles)
7 Tongdean Lane (with bridge
   under railway)
8 South Stand
9 A23 northwards to Crawley
10 To Preston Park railway station
11 North Stand
12 North East Stand
13 West Stand (away)

⬆ *North direction (approx)*

◄ 699849
▼ 699861

bristol city

Ashton Gate Stadium, Ashton Road, Bristol, BS3 2EJ

website: **WWW.BCFC.CO.UK**
e:mail: **ENQUIRIES@BCFC.CO.UK**
tel no: **0871 222 6666**
colours: **RED SHIRTS, WHITE SHORTS**
nickname: **THE ROBINS**
season 2009/10: **CHAMPIONSHIP**

Last Season: **10th** (p**46**; w**15**; d**16**; l**15**; gf**54**; ga**54**)

Having just missed out on promotion at the end of the 2007/08 season, hopes were high at Ashton Gate that City would again feature in the battle for automatic promotion and the Play-Offs. However, with the top of the table largely dominated by a number of clubs recently relegated from the Premier League, who were still benefiting from the parachute payments, Gary Johnson's City found itself top of the chasing pack in early March; however, a late loss of form – which saw the team gain only four points from its last eight League matches without a single win culminating in a 4-0 defeat at Play-Off-chasing Burnley – saw the team slip down the Championship table. The late loss of form will be a cause of concern for City fans and will need addressing if the club is to sustain a challenge again in 2009/10. Although potentially capable of again chasing the Play-Offs, perhaps a top half finish is the best that City can look forward to come the new season.

Tel No: 0117 963 0630
Advance Tickets Tel No: 0871 222 6666
Fax: 0117 963 0700
Training Ground: Queen Elizabeth Hospital's Playing Fields, Clevedon Road, Failand BS8 3TN
Brief History: Founded 1894 as Bristol South End changed to Bristol City in 1897. Former Ground: St John's Lane, Bedminster, moved to Ashton Gate in 1904. Record attendance 43,335
(Total) Current Capacity: 21,479 (all seated)
Visiting Supporters' Allocation: 3,000 in Micra Wedlock Stand (all seated; can be increased to 5,500 if necessary)
Nearest Railway Station: Bristol Temple Meads
Parking (Car): Street parking
Parking (Coach/Bus): Marsh Road
Police Force and Tel No: Avon/Somerset (0117 927 7777)
Disabled Visitors' Facilities:
Wheelchairs: Limited
Blind: Commentary available
Anticipated Development(s): Although the club had previously been planning to redevelop its existing Ashton Gate ground, it was announced in late November 2007 that the club now favoured relocation. The new site, as yet at an undisclosed location close to Ashton Gate, is designed to accommodate a 30,000-seat stadium with the potential to have that increased to 40,000 in the event of the ground forming part of England's bid to host the 2018 World Cup. If all goes according to plan, the club will seek planning permission by the end of 2009 with the new ground available from the start of the 2011/12 season. Following relocation, Ashton Gate is likely to be sold for redevelopment.

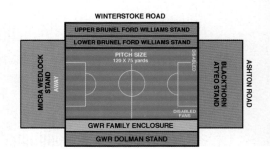

C Club Offices
S Club Shop

1 A370 Ashton Road
2 A3209 Winterstoke Road
3 To Temple Meads Station
   (1½ miles)
4 To City Centre, A4,
   M32 & M4
5 Database Wedlock Stand
6 Atyeo Stand
7 Dolman Stand
8 Brunel Ford Williams Stand

↑ *North direction (approx)*

◀ 702459
▾ 702480

bristol rovers

The Memorial Stadium, Filton Avenue, Horfield, Bristol, BS7 0BF

website: **WWW.BRISTOLROVERS.CO.UK**
e:mail: **FEEDBACK@BRISTOLROVERS.CO.UK**
tel no: **0117 909 6648**
colours: **BLUE AND WHITE QUARTERED SHIRTS, WHITE SHORTS**
nickname: **THE PIRATES (or Gasheads historically)**
season 2009/10: **LEAGUE ONE**

Last Season: **11th** (p**46**; w**17**; d**12**; l**17**; gf**79**; ga**61**)

The Pirates' second season back in League One saw some progress on the field with Paul Trollope's team ultimately achieve a position of mid-table mediocrity. However, the start of the campaign was dire with only one win in the team's first nine League matches and it looked for a time as though Rovers might get drawn into the relegation battle. Placed 19th in the League at the end of September – ironically all four of the teams to be ultimately relegated were already just below Rovers – October proved to be a productive month, with the club winning four out of its five league fixtures. Away from the League, Rovers suffered a 1-0 defeat away at Bournemouth in the First Round of the FA Cup. For 2009/10 it's hard to escape the conclusion that Rovers will again be one of the teams that ultimately fill one of the mid-table positions.

Advance Tickets Tel No: 0117 909 8848

Fax: 0117 908 5530

Training Ground: Bristol Academy of Sport, Filton College, Filton Avenue, Bristol BS34 7AT

Brief History: Founded 1883 as Black Arabs, changed to Eastville Rovers (1884), Bristol Eastville Rovers (1896) and Bristol Rovers (1897). Former grounds: Purdown, Three Acres, The Downs (Horfield), Ridgeway, Bristol Stadium (Eastville), Twerton Park (1986-96), moved to The Memorial Ground 1996. Record attendance: (Eastville) 38,472, (Twerton Park) 9,813, (Memorial Ground) 12,011

(Total) Current Capacity: 11,917; (4,000 seated*)

Visiting Supporters' Allocation: 1,132 (Centenary Uplands Stand Terrace; open)

Nearest Railway Station: Filton or Stapleton Road

Parking (Car): Limited parking at ground for home fans only; street parking also available

Parking (Coach/Bus): As directed

Police Force and Tel No: Avon/Somerset (0117 927 7777)

Other Clubs Sharing Ground: Bristol Shoguns RUFC

Disabled Visitors' Facilities:

Wheelchairs: 35 wheelchair positions

Blind: Limited provision

Anticipated Development(s): The planned redevelopment of the Memorial Ground with the consequent groundshares for Rovers and Bristol RUFC was deferred during the summer of 2008 as a result of the club's partners in the project pulling out of the scheme to construct a new 18,500-seat ground. If all goes according to plan the club now hopes to start work in the summer of 2009 but the original concept of ground-sharing during the construction phase was abandoned. In place the ground will now be redeveloped in phases. The first phase will see the construction of a 7,000-seat stand at the east end to be followed by a new 2,400-seat South Stand. This work is scheduled for completion by the end of the 2009/10 season after which the remaining two stands will be demolished and replacement North and West stands constructed by the end of the 2010/11 season. The entire project is costed at some £35 million.

standing capacity of 8,000 includes 500 on the Family Terrace

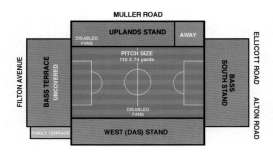

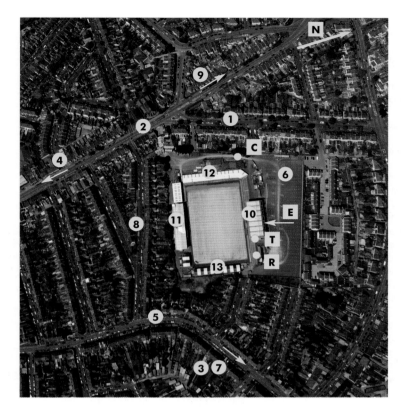

C Rugby Club offices
E Entrance(s) for visiting supporters
R Refrshments for visiting supporters
T Toilets for visiting supporters

1 Filton Avenue
2 Gloucester Road
3 To Muller Road
4 To Bristol city centre (2.5 miles) and BR Temple Meads station (3 miles)
5 Downer Road
6 Car Park
7 To M32 J2 (1½ miles)
8 Strathmore Road
9 To Filton (1½ miles)
10 Uplands Stand
11 West (Das) Stand
12 Becks Stand South
13 South Stand

↑ North direction (approx)

◄ 702490
▼ 702508

burnley

Turf Moor, Harry Potts Way, Burnley, Lancashire, BB10 4BX

website: **WWW.BURNLEYFOOTBALLCLUB.COM**
e:mail: **INFO@BURNLEYFC.COM.**
tel no: **0871 221 1882**
colours: **CLARET AND BLUE SHIRTS, WHITE SHORTS**
nickname: **THE CLARETS**
season 2009/10: **PREMIER LEAGUE**

Last Season: **5th** (promoted) (p**46**; w**21**; d**13**; l**12**; gf**72**; ga**60**)

In Owen Coyle's first full season in charge of Burnley, the Clarets came to have a hugely successful season in both League and Cup competitions, ultimately triumphing in the Play-Off Final to bring top-flight football back to Turf Moor for the first time since relegation at the end of the 1975/76 season. In the intervening 33 years, the club has played in all three of the lower leagues. In the hunt for the Play-Offs for virtually the entire season, it was not until the final game of the season, with a stunning 4-0 victory over Bristol City, that the Play-Offs were ensured. A 1-0 victory in the first leg over Reading combined with an impressive 2-0 victory away set up a final against Sheffield United. The 1-0 win means that for 2009/10 Burnley will face local derbies against teams like Bolton, Blackburn and the two Manchester clubs. Away from the League, the team also repeated its considerable success from 2007/08, beating Fulham 1-0 in the Third Round of the Carling Cup, Chelsea at Stamford Bridge in the Fourth Round on penalties (when the match had ended 1-1 after extra time) and Arsenal 2-0 in the Quarter Finals before losing to Spurs in the Semi-Final. In the FA Cup, victory over West Brom 3-1 in the Fourth Round set up another match against Arsenal, although this time the Londoners ran out 3-0 winners. For 2009/10, Burnley will undoubtedly start as one of the pre-season favourites to make an immediate return to the Championship, but the club's success against Premier League opposition in the Cup competitions will give fans hope that the team can emulate the success of other promoted teams like Stoke and Hull and survive at least one season.

Advanced Tickets No: 0871 221 1916
Fax: 01282 700014
Training Ground: Gawthorpe Hall, off Padiham Road, Padiham, Burnley BB12 8UA
Brief History: Founded 1882, Burnley Rovers (Rugby Club) combined with another Rugby Club, changed to soccer and name to Burnley. Moved from Calder Vale to Turf Moor in 1882. Founder-members Football League (1888). Record attendance 54,775
(Total) Current Capacity: 22,546 all seated)
Visiting Supporters' Allocation: 2,500 in lower tier of Jimmy McIlroy Stand
Nearest Railway Station: Burnley Central
Parking (Car): Church Street and Fulledge Rec. (car parks)
Parking (Coach/Bus): As directed by Police
Police Force and Tel No: Lancashire (01282 425001)
Disabled Visitors' Facilities:
Wheelchairs: Places available in North, East and Cricket Field stands
Blind: Headsets provided with commentary
Anticipated Development(s): Planning Permission was granted in late June 2008 for the first phase in the redevelopment of Turf Moor. This will see the construction of a new two-storey building behind the Jimmy McIlroy and Jimmy Hargreaves stands. It is planned that work on the reconstruction of the Cricket Field (David Fishwick) Stand will commence after the end of the 2008/09 season. The new structure will be a single-tier stand accommodating 2,500 costing £10 million. During the stand's construction, away fans will be housed in the lower tier of the Jimmy McIlroy Stand. This work will be followed by the refurbishment of the Bob Lord Stand.

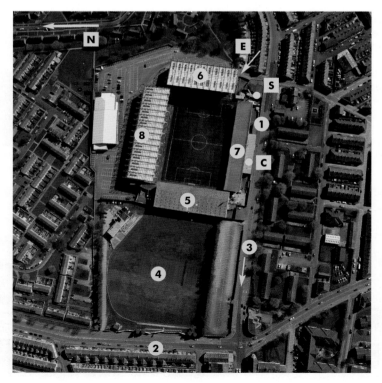

701945
701933

C Club Offices
S Club Shop
E Entrance(s) for visiting
supporters

1 Brunshaw Road
2 Belvedere Road
3 Burnley Central BR Station
(½ mile)
4 Cricket Ground
5 Cricket Field Stand
6 East (Jimmy McIlroy) Stand
7 Bob Lord Stand
8 North (James Hargreaves)
Stand

↑ *North direction (approx)*

burton albion

Pirelli Stadium, Princess Way, Burton-on-Trent, Staffordshire DE13 0AR

website: **WWW.BURTONALBIONFC.CO.UK**
e:mail: **BAFC@BURTONALBIONFC.CO.UK**
telephone: **01283 565938**
colours: **YELLOW SHIRTS, BLACK SHORTS**
Nickname: **THE BREWERS**
season 2009/10: **LEAGUE TWO**

Last Season: **1st** (promoted) (p**46**; w **27**; d **7**; l **12**; gf **81**; ga **52**)

For much of the season it looked as though Burton Albion would become the fourth club from England's brewing capital to enter the Football League as the team, initially under long-term manager Nigel Clough (until his departure to take over at Derby County in January 2009) and then his successor Roy McFarland, romped into an 11-point lead with seven games remaining. However, a late loss of form – that saw the Brewers lose five of the remaining matches – allowed Cambridge United to close to within three points and ensure a tense final weekend. Although Albion had the better goal difference, the team faced a tricky away match at Play-Off chasing Torquay United, whilst Cambridge faced a home match against Altrincham. Although Albion lost 2-1 at Plainmoor, a 0-0 draw at Cambridge ensured that League football will be on offer at the Pirelli Stadium in 2009/10. Following the end of the campaign, it was confirmed that McFarland did not wish to remain as manager, although he was happy to assist any new appointment, and new boss Paul Peschisolido will face trying to keep the Brewers up. Unusually, it has been decided that Albion's players will retain their part-time status. Whilst this is probably sound financially, it will be a handicap on the field. Potentially, therefore, it could be a tricky season for Albion to stay up – previous teams from Burton have never prospered long in the League – and a battle to avoid the drop looks to be on the cards.

Advance Tickets Tel No: 01283 565938
Fax: 01283 523199
Training Ground: None
Brief History: Burton Albion was founded in 1950 and was promoted to the Football League at the end of the 2008/09 season. Achieving League status means that it is the fourth club from Burton to achieve this feat, following from Burton Swifts (1892-1902), Burton Wanderers (1894-97) and Burton United (1901-07). Previous grounds: Lloyds Foundry and Eton Park (1958-2005). Record attendance (Pirelli Stadium): 6,191
(Total) Current Capacity: 6,912 (2,034 seated)
Visiting Supporters' Allocation:
Nearest Railway Station: Burton-on-Trent (½ mile)
Parking (Car): 400 places at the ground with overflow at adjacent Rykneld Trading Estate
Parking (Coach/Bus): As directed
Police Force and Tel No: Staffordshire (0300 123 4455)
Disabled Visitors' Facilities:
Wheelchairs:
Blind:

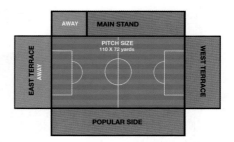

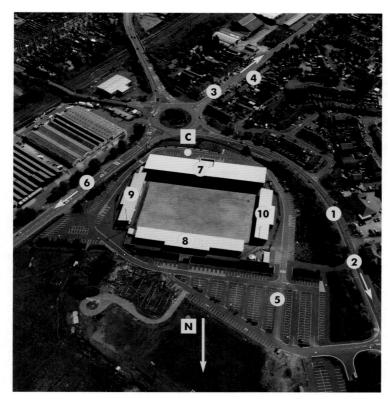

C   Club offices

1   Princess Way
2   To A38
3   A5121 Derby Road
4   To Burton town centre and railway station
5   Car park
6   To A38 and Derby
7   Main Stand
8   Popular Side
9   East Terrace (Away)
10 West Terrace

↑   North direction (approx)

◄ 702609
▼ 702639

bury

Gigg Lane, Gigg Lane, Bury, Lancashire, BL9 9HR

website: **WWW.BURYFC.CO.UK**
e:mail: **INFO@BURYFC.CO.UK**
tel no: **0161 764 4881**
colours: **WHITE SHIRTS, ROYAL BLUE SHORTS**
nickname: **THE SHAKERS**
season 2009/10: **LEAGUE TWO**

Last Season: **4th** (p**46**; w**21**; d**15**; l**10**; gf**63**; ga**43**)

Ultimately a hugely disappointing season for Alan Knill and his Bury team, the Shakers were in the hunt for automatic promotion for much of the season and right up until the final day the team was in with an opportunity of snatching third place from Wycombe Wanderers. Needing a victory over Accrington Stanley and a defeat for Wanderers by lowly Notts County, both results went in Bury's favour but a failure to score more than a 1-0 victory over Stanley meant that Wycombe held onto third spot and consigned Bury to the Play-Offs. A 1-0 away win at seventh-placed Shrewsbury seemed to give Bury the edge – particularly as Shrewsbury had an appalling away record in the League – but the return game at Gigg Lane turned into match of real drama as the Shrews scored a late goal to take the match to extra time. Playing for the bulk of extra time with 10 players, Shrewsbury hung on to force the match to penalties in which the Shropshire side was to triumph 4-3. Thus Bury face another season of League Two football but, provided they can put the disappointment of 2008/09 behind them, the Shakers should again be one of the teams vying for the Play-Offs at least in 2009/10.

Advance Tickets Tel No: 0161 705 2144
Fax: 0161 764 5521
Training Ground: Lower Gigg, Gigg Lane, Bury BL9 9HR
Brief History: Founded 1885, no former names or former grounds. Record attendance 35,000
(Total) Current Capacity: 11,669 (all seated)
Visiting Supporters' Allocation: 2,000 (all seated) in Manchester Road Stand
Nearest Railway Station: Bury Interchange
Parking (Car): Street parking
Parking (Coach/Bus): As directed by Police
Police Force and Tel No: Greater Manchester (0161 872 5050)
Other clubs sharing ground:
FC United of Manchester
Disabled Visitors' Facilities:
Wheelchairs: South Stand (home) and West Stand (away)
Blind: Commentary available
Anticipated Development(s): The completion of the rebuilt Cemetery End means that current plans for the redevelopment of Gigg Lane have been completed.

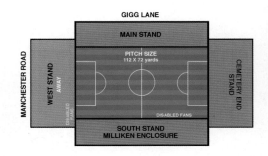

C Club Offices
S Club Shop

1 Car Park
2 Gigg Lane
3 A56 Manchester Road
4 To Town Centre & Bury
  Interchange (Metrolink)
  (¾ mile)
5 West (Manchester Road)
  Stand (away)
6 Cemetery End

↑ North direction (approx)

◄ 701853
▼ 701863

cardiff city

Cardiff City Ground, Leckwith Road, Cardiff

website: **WWW.CARDIFFCITYFC.CO.UK**
e:mail: **CLUB@CARDIFFCITYFC.CO.UK**
tel no: **029 2022 1001***
colours: **BLUE SHIRTS, BLUE SHORTS**
nickname: **THE BLUEBIRDS**
season 2009/10: **CHAMPIONSHIP**

Last Season: **7th** (p**46**; w**19**; d**17**; l**10**; gf**65**; ga**53**)

In the Bluebirds' final season at its historic Ninian Park ground prior to the move to the new Cardiff City Stadium, there was considerable hope that the club would make a sustained push for either promotion or the Play-Offs. Under Dave Jones the club was in the hunt for the latter for much of the season and retained an outside chance of automatic promotion until mid-April. However, from 13 April, when the team stood in fourth place with a Play-Off place looking almost certain, a late loss of form – which saw the Bluebirds gain only one point from a possible 12 – resulted in the team ultimately finishing a disappointing seventh. Ultimately, it came down to the last game of the season. Provided that City at least drew at Sheffield Wednesday, Preston's result against QPR became irrelevant. In the event Preston won 2-1 and Cardiff lost 1-0. The net result was that both teams finished on 74 points with an identical goal difference; Preston gained the all-important sixth place as a result of having scored more goals. Consigned again to Championship football, the boost that the new stadium gives the team may well be a factor in enabling the team to make a more sustained challenge in 2009/10.

Advance Tickets Tel No: 0845 345 1400*
Fax: 029 2034 1148*
Training Ground: University of Glamorgan, Tyn-Y-Wern Playing Fields, Treforest Industrial Estate, Upper Boat, Pontypridd, CF37 5UP
Brief History: Founded 1899. Former grounds: Riverside Cricket Club, Roath, Sophia Gardens, Cardiff Arms Park and Ninian Park from 1910. Moved to new Cardiff City Stadium in August 2009. Ground record attendance (Ninian Park): 61,566 (Wales v. England, 1961)
(Total) Current Capacity: 26,828
Visiting Supporters' Allocation: tbc
Nearest Railway Station: Ninian Park (adjacent); Cardiff Central (one mile)
Parking (Car): Adjacent to ground
Parking (Coach/Bus): as directed
Other clubs sharing Ground: Cardiff Blues RUFC
Police Force and Tel No: South Wales (029 2022 2111)
Disabled Visitors' Facilities:
Wheelchairs: tbc
Blind: tbc
Anticipated Development(s): Following the completion of the new £42 million stadium, the club relocated from its old ground at Ninian Park for the start of the 2009/10 season.

*These are the numbers for Ninian Park and may change with the relocation

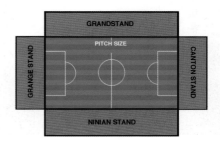

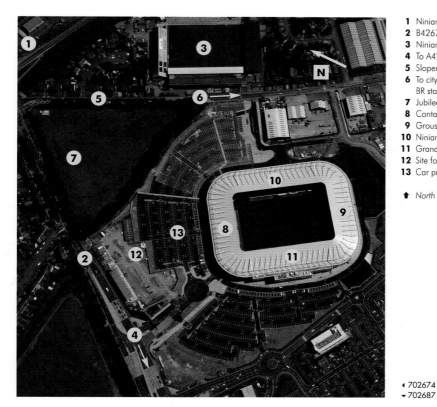

1 Ninian Park BR station
2 B4267 Leckwith Road
3 Ninian Park (old ground)
4 To A4232 Grangetown Link
5 Sloper Road
6 To city centre and Central
  BR station
7 Jubilee Park
8 Contan Stand
9 Grouse Stand
10 Ninian Stand
11 Grandstand
12 Site for future hotel
13 Car parks

⬆ *North direction (approx)*

◀ 702674
▼ 702687

carlisle united

Brunton Park, Warwick Road, Carlisle, CA1 1LL

website: **WWW.CARLISLEUNITED.CO.UK**
e:mail: **ENQUIRIES@CARLISLEUNITED.CO.UK**
tel no: **01228 526237**
colours: **BLUE SHIRTS, WHITE SHORTS**
nickname: **THE CUMBRIANS OR THE BLUES**
season 2009/10: **LEAGUE ONE**

Last season **20th** (p**46** w**12** d**14** l**20** gf**56** ga**69**)

Having just missed out in the Play-offs at the end of the 2007/08 season, confidence was high at Brunton Park that the 2008/09 season would again see the Cumbrians challenge for the Play-Offs at the very least and, despite the sale of two key players – Kieren Westwood and Joe Garner – before the start of the campaign, early results, with the team unbeaten in the League during August seemed positive. Things soon started to go wrong, however. As the club gradually drifted down the League One table, manager John Ward – appointed in the autumn of 2007 – departed the club 'by mutual consent' in early November to be replaced by Greg Abbott. Initially appointed as caretaker, Abbott was confirmed as permanent manager later in the season. Under Abbott's stewardship, the club retained its League One status although it took a 2-0 home victory over promotion-chasing Millwall on the last Saturday to confirm survival. One of four teams realistically in with a shout of filling the final relegation spot – Crewe were effectively already relegated as a result of their poor goal difference – United started the day in 21st position. However, the home victory, combined with Northampton's defeat at Leeds, was sufficient to consign the Cobblers to League Two. For 2009/10 the club – under new ownership since the summer of 2008 – has the potential to again challenge for the Play-Offs at least but a position mid-table may be a more realistic aspiration.

Advance Tickets Tel No: 0844 371 1921
Fax: 01228 554141
Training Ground: Adjacent to main ground
Brief History: Founded 1904 as Carlisle United (previously named Shaddongate United). Former Grounds: Millholme Bank and Devonshire Park, moved to Brunton Park in 1909. Record attendance 27,500
(Total) Current Capacity: 16,981 (6,433 seated)
Visiting Supporters' Allocation: 1,700 (Petterill End Terrace – open – or north end of Main Cumberland Building Society Stand)
Nearest Railway Station: Carlisle
Parking (Car): Rear of ground
Parking (Coach/Bus): St Aiden's Road car park
Police Force and Tel No: Cumbria (01228 528191)
Disabled Visitors' Facilities:
Wheelchairs: East Stand and Paddock (prior arrangement)
Blind: No special facilities
Anticipated Development(s):

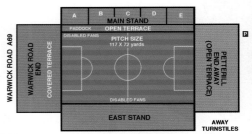

48

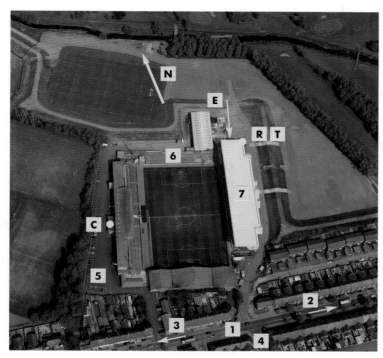

C Club Offices
E Entrance(s) for visiting supporters
R Refreshment bars for visiting supporters
T Toilets for visiting supporters

1 A69 Warwick Road
2 To M6 Junction 43
3 Carlisle Citadel BR station (1 mile)
4 Greystone Road
5 Car Park
6 Petterill End (away)
7 Cumberland Bulding Society (East) Stand

⬆ North direction (approx)

◀ 701256
▾ 701264

charlton athletic

The Valley, Floyd Road, Charlton, London, SE7 8BL

website: **WWW.CAFC.CO.UK**
e:mail: **CUSTOMERSERVICES@CAFC.CO.UK**
tel no: **020 8333 4000**
colours: **RED SHIRTS, WHITE SHORTS**
nickname: **THE ADDICKS**
season 2009/10: **LEAGUE ONE**

Last Season: **24th** (Relegated) (p**46**; w**8**; d**15**; l**23**; gf**52**; ga**74**)

A hugely disappointing season saw the Addicks relegated to the third tier of English football for the first time since the 1980/81 season. In the club's second season back in the League Championship following relegation from the Premier League at the end of the 2006/07 season, fans were expecting Alan Pardew to build on the 2007/08 season and push towards the Play-Offs at least, particularly as this was the last of the two seasons in which the Addicks could expect the parachute payments from the Premier League. In the event, a poor start to the season, culminating in a 5-2 home reverse against Sheffield United in late November, which left the Addicks in 22nd position, resulted in Pardew's departure and the appointment of his assistant, Phil Parkinson, as manager initially on a caretaker basis but made full-time later. Ironically, although the two teams at that stage below Charlton – Doncaster and Forest – ultimately survived, Charlton's form continued to deteriorate and relegation was confirmed well before the end of the season. Ironically, the club's best form came towards the end of the season with a run of two wins and five draws in the last eight games. The last time that the Addicks were relegated to the old Third Division, they were promoted back immediately. The team ought to have the pedigree to achieve the same this time round, but it may well be a struggle and the Play-Offs may well be the best that the fans can hope for.

Advance Tickets Tel No: 0871 226 1905
Fax: 020 8333 4001
Training Ground: Sparrows Lane, New Eltham, London SE9 2JR
Brief History: Founded 1905. Former grounds: Siemens Meadows, Woolwich Common, Pound Park, Angerstein Athletic Ground, The Mount Catford, Selhurst Park (Crystal Palace FC), Boleyn Ground (West Ham United FC), The Valley (1912-23, 1924-85, 1992-date). Founder Members 3rd Division South. Record attendance 75,031
(Total) Current Capacity: 27,111 (all seated)
Visiting Supporters' Allocation: 3,000 (maximum; all seated in South Stand)
Nearest Railway Station: Charlton
Parking (Car): Street parking
Parking (Coach/Bus): As directed by Police
Police Force and Tel No: Metropolitan (020 8853 8212)
Disabled Visitors' Facilities:
Wheelchairs: East/West/South stands
Blind: Commentary, 12 spaces
Anticipated Development(s): The club has Planning Permission for the redevelopment of the East Stand, taking the ground's capacity to 31,000 but there is no confirmed timescale for the work. In December 2006 the club also lodged outline plans for the redevelopment of the rest of the stadium with the intention of taking capacity to 40,600.

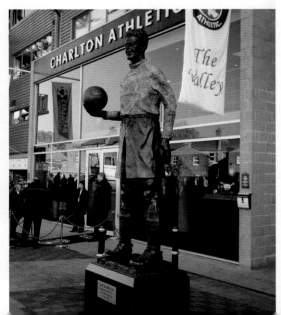

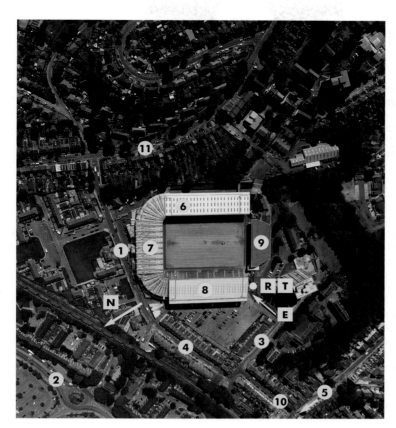

E Entrance(s) for visiting supporters

R Refreshment bars for visiting supporters

T Toilets for visiting supporters

1 Harvey Gardens
2 A206 Woolwich Road
3 Valley Grove
4 Floyd Road
5 Charlton BR Station
6 East Stand
7 North Stand
8 West stand
9 South stand (away)
10 Charlton Church Lane
11 Charlton Lane

⬆ *North direction (approx)*

◄ 701309
▼ 701316

chelsea

Stamford Bridge, Fulham Road, London, SW6 1HS

website: **WWW.CHELSEAFC.COM**
e:mail: **CONTACT VIA WEBSITE**
tel no: **0871 984 1955**
colours: **BLUE SHIRTS, BLUE SHORTS**
nickname: **THE BLUES**
season 2009/10: **PREMIER LEAGUE**

Last Season: **3rd** (p**38**; w**25**; d**8**; l**5**; gf**68**; ga**24**)

With a manager proven to have had success at the highest level in Luiz Felipe Scolari, expectations were high at Stamford Bridge that the club now had a boss capable of fulfilling Roman Abramovich's aspirations. The start of Scolari's era was promising but the gloss faded when the club lost at home to Liverpool in the League – the club's first League defeat at Stamford Bridge in 87 matches – and on penalties to Championship side Burnley in the Fourth Round of the Carling Cup. The end of Scolari's reign was swift; sacked in early February, he was almost immediately replaced by Guus Hiddink, who combined the job with continuing as boss of Russia. From the start it was stated that Hiddink would stay only until the end of the season but under him the club's form improved, reaching the Semi-Finals of the Champions League – where they were knocked out in controversial circumstances at Stamford Bridge by eventual winners Barcelona – and the FA Cup Final, where Chelsea faced Everton. Conceding the fastest goal ever scored in the Cup Final was not perhaps the best start but Hiddink's team equalised before half time and went on to dominate the second half before emerging as 2-1 victors. Thus the Hiddink era ended with silverware at Stamford Bridge and new boss Carlo Ancelotti from AC Milan will inherit a club with renewed spirit. Chelsea will again be expected to challenge Manchester United for the title but one of the cup competitions is again perhaps a more realistic hope.

Advance Tickets Tel No: 0871 984 1905

Fax: 020 7381 4831

Training Ground: 62 Stoke Road, Cobham, Surrey KT11 3PT

Brief History: Founded 1905. Admitted to Football League (2nd Division) on formation. Stamford Bridge venue for F.A. Cup Finals 1919-22. Record attendance 82,905

(Total Current Capacity: 42,449 (all seated)

Visiting Supporters' Allocation: Approx. 1,600 (East Stand Lower; can be increased to 3,200 if required or 5,200 if part of the Matthew Harding Stand [lower tier] is allocated)

Nearest Railway Station: Fulham Broadway or West Brompton

Parking (Car): Street parking and underground car park at ground

Parking (Coach/Bus): As directed by Police

Police Force and Tel No: Metropolitan (020 7385 1212)

Disabled Visitors' Facilities:

Wheelchairs: East Stand

Blind: No special facility

Anticipated Development(s): Faced by the competing clubs building ever larger grounds, Chelsea is conscious that the existing 42,000-seat capacity at Stamford Bridge is too small but difficult to increase. As a result the club is examining the possibility of relocation, with a number of sites (including the erstwhile Lillie Bridge cricket ground now used as the Seagrave Road car park as one option). There is, however, no definite plan as yet nor any timetable for the work if it were to proceed.

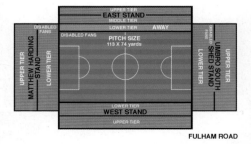

FULHAM ROAD

N

1 A304 Fulham Road
2 To Central London
3 Fulham Broadway
   Tube Station
4 Matthew Harding Stand
5 East Stand
6 West Stand
7 South (Shed) Stand
8 West Brompton Station

↑ *North direction (approx)*

◀ 701425
▼ 701421

cheltenham town

Abbey Business Stadium, Whaddon Road, Cheltenham, Gloucestershire GL52 5NA

website: **WWW.CTFC.COM**
e:mail: **INFO@CTFC.COM**
tel no: **01242 573558**
colours: **RED AND WHITE STRIPED SHIRTS, WHITE SHORTS**
nickname: **THE ROBINS**
season 2009/10: **LEAGUE TWO**

Last Season: **23rd** (relegated) (p**46**; w**9**; d**12**; l**25**; gf**51**; ga**91**)

Following a 4-1 defeat by Hartlepool United – a result that left Town rooted to the bottom of the League Two table – Keith Downing was sacked as boss. He'd held the full time job for less than a year, although he'd been caretaker prior to that date and had been instrumental in ensuring that the club didn't get relegated at the end of the 2007/08 season. The club moved quickly to appoint the experienced Martin Allen, out of the game since leaving Leicester City in late 2007, to the vacancy. However, under Allen the club continued to struggle, losing six League games on the trot between the middle of October and the end of November and seven between the end of January and the end of February. Rooted in the drop zone for virtually the entire season, it came as no surprise when the Robins' relegation back to League Two was confirmed at the end of April following a 1-1 draw at Whaddon Road against fellow strugglers Carlisle United. The club's financial problems – it narrowly averted Administration during the season – and the likely reduction in the squad for the 2009/10 mean that the new season could well see the club face a serious battle to retain its League status.

Advance Tickets Tel No: 01242 573558
Fax: 01242 224675
Training Ground: Cheltenham Town FC Training Complex, Quat Goose Lane, Swindon Village, Cheltenham GL51 9RX
Brief History: Cheltenham Town was founded in 1892. It moved to Whaddon Road in 1932 having previously played at Carter's Field. After two seasons in the Conference it achieved Nationwide League status at the end of the 1998/99 season. Record attendance 8,326
(Total Current Capacity:: 7,066 (3,912 seated)
Visiting Supporters' Allocation: 2,000 all-seated in Wymans Road (In2Print) Stand plus up to 600 seats in Whaddon Road (Carlsberg) Stand if required
Nearest Railway Station:
Cheltenham (1.5 miles)
Parking (Car): Limited parking at ground; otherwise on-street
Parking (Coach/Bus): As directed by Police
Police Force and Tel No: Gloucestershire (01242 521321)
Disabled Visitors' Facilities:
Wheelchairs: 68 wheelchair spaces
Blind: No special facility
Anticipated Development(s): The Carlsberg stand – which replaced the open Whaddon Road Terrace – was opened in December 2005. This structure provides seats for 1,000 fans. The next phase in the development of Whaddon Road will involve the rebuilding of the Main Stand, but there is at present no timescale for this work.

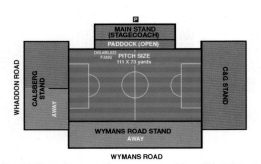

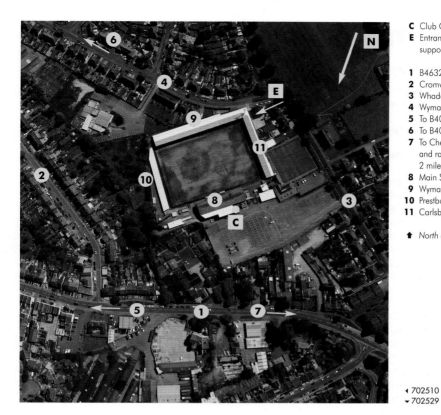

C Club Offices
E Entrance(s) for visiting
    supporters

1 B4632 Prestbury Road
2 Cromwell Road
3 Whaddon Road
4 Wymans Road
5 To B4075 Priors Road
6 To B4075 Prior Road
7 To Cheltenham town centre
    and railway station (1.5 and
    2 miles respectively)
8 Main Stand
9 Wymans Road Stand
10 Prestbury Road End
11 Carlsberg Stand (away)

⬆ *North direction (approx)*

◀ 702510
▼ 702529

chesterfield

Recreation Ground, Saltergate, Chesterfield, S40 4SX

website: **WWW.CHESTERFIELD-FC.CO.UK**
e:mail: **SUEGREEN@CHESTERFIELD-FC.CO.UK**
tel no: **01246 209765**
colours: **BLUE AND WHITE SHIRTS, WHITE SHORTS**
nickname: **THE SPIREITES**
season 2009/10: **LEAGUE TWO**

Last Season: **10th** (p**46**; w**16**; d**15**; l**15**; gf**62**; ga**57**)

Under Lee Richardson, the Spireites ultimately had a disappointing season. Having just missed the Play-Offs at the end of the 2007/08 season, hopes were high at Saltergate that the team would do considerably better in 2008/09. A modest start to the season resulted in the team seemingly marooned in mid-table for much of the campaign but a surge towards the end of March saw the team up to ninth with games in hand over both the three teams directly ahead and the momentum seemed to indicate that the team was a dark horse for the final Play-Off place. In the event, however, the final eight games saw a run of five draws and three defeats and the club ultimately finished a disappointing 10th. With Richardson no longer in charge – his contract was not renewed at the end of the season – the new manager, John Sheridan, will face a challenge if Chesterfield are to be in the hunt for automatic promotion. Perhaps the Play-Offs are again the best that can be hoped for.

Advance Tickets Tel No: 01246 209765
Fax: 01246 556799
Training Ground: No special facility
Brief History: Found 1886. Former Ground: Spital Vale. Formerly named Chesterfield Town. Record attendance 30,968
(Total) Current Capacity: 8,504 (2,674 seated)
Visiting Supporters' Allocation: 1,850 maximum (maximum 450 seated)
Nearest Railway Station: Chesterfield
Parking (Car): Saltergate car park, street parking
Parking (Coach/Bus): As directed by Police
Police Force and Tel No: Derbyshire (01246 220100)
Disabled Visitors' Facilities:
Wheelchairs: Saltergate Stand
Blind: No special facility
Anticipated Development(s): Planning consent for the Spireites' new 10,500-seat ground was granted in July 2008 with the intention of being completed by the start of the 2010/11 season. The £13 million scheme, which also involves a Tesco supermarket, will be constructed on the site of the erstwhile Demaglass works. Once the club relocates the old ground at Saltergate will be redeveloped for residential purposes.

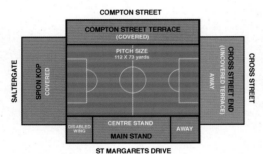

C Club Offices
S Club Shop
E Entrance(s) for visiting
    supporters
R Refreshment bars for visiting
    supporters
T Toilets for visiting supporters

1 Saltergate
2 Cross Street
3 St Margaret's Drive
4 West Bars
5 To A617 & M1 Junction 29
6 To station and town centre
7 Compton Street Terrace
8 Cross Street End (away)

↑ *North direction (approx)*

◄ 701043
▼ 701047

colchester united

Weston Homes Community Stadium, United Way, Colchester CO4 5UP

website: **WWW.CU–FC.COM**
e:mail: **CAROLINE@COLCHESTERUNITED.NET**
tel no: **01206 755100**
colours: **BLUE AND WHITE SHIRTS, WHITE SHORTS**
nickname: **THE U'S**
season 2009/10: **LEAGUE ONE**

Last Season: **12th** (p**46**; w**18**; d**9**; l**19**; gf**58**; ga**58**)

The preseason optimism engendered by the opening of the club's new ground soon disappeared as the club struggled to find its feet in League One following its relegation at the end of the 2007/08 season. Geraint Williams was to depart as manager in late September with the club, after a 3-0 defeat by MK Dons, sitting second from bottom in the table. Following a brief period in which Kit Symons acted as caretaker boss, Paul Lambert was appointed the new manager in early October; a measure of the task facing him was shown in his first game in charge when United contrived to lose 4-3 at fellow strugglers Cheltenham Town having been 3-1 up. Under Lambert, the club's form improved and the team gradually rose up the League One table, ultimately finishing in 12th position. The position might have been even better save for a late loss of form that saw the team lose six of its last 10 League games and thus throw away a late shout at the Play-Offs. For 2009/10, United ought to have the potential for another top-half finish with the outside chance of the Play-Offs.

Advance Tickets Tel No: 0871 226 2161
Fax: 01206 755 114
Training Ground: No special facility
Brief History: Founded 1937, joined Football League 1950, relegated 1990 to Conference, promoted back to the Football League 1992. Played at Layer Road until end of 2007/08 season. Record attendance (at Layer Road) 19,072; (at Weston Homes Community Stadium) 9,559
(Total) Current Capacity: 10,000 (all seated)
Visiting Supporters' Allocation: 1,832 (South Stand)
Nearest Railway Station: Colchester main line (two miles)
Parking (Car): 600 spaces at ground
Parking (Coach/Bus): As directed
Police Force and Tel No: Essex (01206 762212)
Disabled Visitors' Facilities:
Wheelchairs: 100 wheelchair places
Blind: No special facility
Anticipated Development(s): Following a number of years planning for relocation, the club played its final season at its old Layer Road ground in 2007/08 and relocated to the new £14 million 10,000-seat stadium for the start of the 2008/09 campaign. The ground is designed to allow for expansion to 18,000 if the need arises.

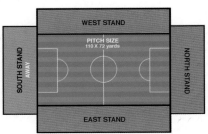

1 A12
2 Towards intersection with new northern link road and Ipswich
3 Towards London
4 To Colchester town centre (three miles) and Colchester main line station
5 North Stand
6 East Stand
7 West Stand
8 South Stand

↑ North direction (approx)

◄ 701440
▼ 701468

coventry city

The Ricoh Arena, Phoenix Way, Foleshill, Coventry CV6 6GE

website: **WWW.CCFC.CO.UK**
e:mail: **CUSTOMER.SERVICES@CCFC.CO.UK**
tel no: **0844 873 1883**
colours: **SKY BLUE SHIRTS, SKY BLUE SHORTS**
nickname: **THE SKY BLUES**
season 2009/10: **CHAMPIONSHIP**

Last Season: **17th** (p**46**; w**13**; d**15**; l**18**; gf**47**; ga**58**)

Under Chris Coleman City had a disappointing season with the possibility that the club might get drawn into the battle to avoid the drop once again. Mid-table at the end of February, a dire run towards the end of the campaign saw the Sky Blues win only one and draw four of the club's last 13 League matches. For a team like Coventry, no longer buttressed by the Premier League parachute payments, it is salutary to note that the three teams relegated at the end of the 2008/09 season – Charlton, Norwich and Southampton – are also teams that have been relegated recently from the Premier League. The Championship is no respecter of reputations and it's either an immediate bounce back or a serious struggle to stay in the Championship. City are now in the 'serious struggle' phase and there is a danger that, unless early season form shows a considerable improvement on that experienced at the back end of the past season, Coventry could be staring at a further battle against the drop.

Advance Tickets Tel No: 0844 873 1883
Fax: 0844 873 6301
Training Ground: Sky Blue Lodge, Leamington Road, Ryton-on-Dunsmore, Coventry CV8 3EL
Brief History: Founded 1883 as Singers FC, changed name to Coventry City in 1898. Former grounds: Dowell's Field, Stoke Road Ground and Highfield Road (1899-2005) moved to new ground for start of the 2005/06 season. Record attendance (at Highfield Road): 51,455; (at Ricoh Arena): 31,407
(Total) Current Capacity: 32,500 (All seated)
Visiting Supporters' Allocation: 3,000 in corner of Jewson South and Telnet West Stands
Nearest Railway Station: Coventry (three miles)
Parking (Car): As directed
Parking (Coach/Bus): As directed
Police Force and Tel No: West Midlands (02476 539010)
Disabled Visitors' Facilities:
Wheelchairs: 102 spaces (including 27 away) at pitchside or raised platform
Blind: no special facility at present but under negotiation
Anticipated Development(s): With the completion of the Ricoh Stadium there are no further plans for development at the present time. There is still no news about the construction of a possible station on the Coventry-Nuneaton railway line.

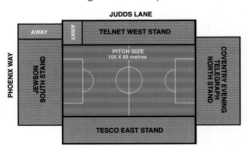

JUDDS LANE

AWAY | AWAY | TELNET WEST STAND

PHOENIX WAY

JEWSON SOUTH STAND

PITCH SIZE
105 X 68 metres

COVENTRY EVENING TELEGRAPH NORTH STAND

TESCO EAST STAND

▲ 702554
◀ 702564

N

1 Judds Lane
2 Rowley's Green Lane
3 A444 Phoenix Way
4 To Coventry city centre
  and BR railway station
  (three miles)
5 Coventry-Nuneaton
  railway line
6 To M6 Junction 3 (one mile)
  and Nuneaton
7 Telnet West Stand
8 Coventry Evening Telegraph
  North Stand
9 Tesco East Stand
10 Jewson South Stand
11 Exhibition hall and
   planned casino

↑ *North direction (approx)*

crewe alexandra

The Alexandra Stadium, Gresty Road, Crewe, Cheshire, CW2 6EB

website: **WWW.CREWEALEX.NET**
e:mail: **INFO@CREWEALEX.NET**
tel no: **01270 213014**
colours: **RED SHIRTS, WHITE SHORTS**
nickname: **THE RAILWAYMEN**
season 2009/10: **LEAGUE TWO**

Last Season: **22nd** (relegated) (p**46**; w**12**; d**10**; l**24**; gf**59**; ga**82**)

Having just avoided relegation in his first season in charge, Steve Holland spent heavily in the close season although the incoming players were countered by the departure of prolific striker Nicky Maynard to Bristol City. However, despite the promise of the pre-season, the League campaign started disastrously with the Railwaymen taking only nine points from the first 16 matches. Holland was relieved of his duties in November 2008 with ex-boss Dario Gradi temporarily retaking the reins until the appointment of Gudjon Thordarson as the new manager until the end of the season during the following month. Under Thordarson the club battled hard to retain its League One status and by the middle of March had pulled well clear of the drop zone with a six-point margin between it and 21st position. However, a run of five draws and five defeats in the final 10 League games resulted in the club being all but relegated before the final match of the season. Needing results to go their way and to defeat Champions Leicester by a virtual cricket score, a 3-0 home defeat consigned Crewe back to League Two for the first time in more than a decade. As a relegated team Crewe – under manager Thordarson again – should have the potential to make a serious bid for the Play-Offs at the very least.

Advance Tickets Tel No: 01270 252610
Fax: 01270 216320
Training Ground: Details omitted at club's request
Brief History: Founded 1877. Former Grounds: Alexandra Recreation Ground (Nantwich Road), Earle Street Cricket Ground, Edleston Road, Old Sheds Fields, Gresty Road (Adjacent to current Ground), moved to current Ground in 1906. Founder members of 2nd Division (1892) until 1896. Founder members of 3rd Division North (1921). Record attendance 20,000
(Total) Current Capacity: 10,066 (all seated)
Visiting Supporters' Allocation: 1,694 (Blue Bell BMW Stand)
Nearest Railway Station: Crewe
Parking (car): There is a car park adjacent to the ground. It should be noted that there is a residents' only scheme in operation in the streets surrounding the ground.
Parking (Coach/Bus): As directed by Police
Police Force and Tel No: Cheshire (01270 500222)
Disabled Visitors' Facilities:
Wheelchairs: Available on all four sides
Blind: Commentary available
Anticipated Development(s): The club has long term plans for the construction of a new two-tier stand to replace the Blue Bell (BMW) Stand, although there is no confirmed timescale for the work.

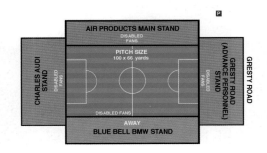

C Club Offices
S Club Shop
E Entrance(s) for visiting
   supporters

1 Crewe BR Station
2 Gresty Road
3 Gresty Road
4 A534 Nantwich Road
5 To A5020 to
   M6 Junction 16
6 To M6 Junction 17 [follow
   directions at roundabout to
   M6 J16/J17]
7 Main (Air Products) Stand
8 Gresty Road (Advance
   Personnel) Stand
9 Charles Audi Stand
10 Ringways Stand
   (Blue Bell BMW)(away)
11 Car Park

↑ North direction (approx)

◄ 700949
▼ 700955

crystal palace

Selhurst Park Stadium, Whitehorse Lane, London, SE25 6PU

website: **WWW.CPFC.CO.UK**
e:mail: **INFO@CPFC.CO.UK**
tel no: **020 8768 6000**
colours: **BLUE AND RED STRIPED SHIRTS, BLUE SHORTS**
nickname: **THE EAGLES (historically the Glaziers)**
season 2009/10: **CHAMPIONSHIP**

Last Season: **15th** (w**15**; d**12**; l**19**; gf**52**; ga**55**)

A poor start to the season, including a crushing 4-0 defeat away at League One Leeds United in the Second Round of the Carling Cup, seemed to set the tempo for Crystal Palace's year. After eight games, with only a single League win, the Eagles were rooted in the bottom three but a run of form mid-season took Neil Warnock's team up to the heights of sixth on Boxing Day – it certainly looked as though Christmas had arrived for Eagles fans! However, this form was not to be perpetuated and the New Year brought a run of only four wins and five draws in the club's final 21 League games – form which might have brought relegation if it had been consistently repeated throughout the season. Warnock is a highly experienced manager but with finance at the club tight it will be hard for him to build a team capable of mounting a serious challenge in 2009/10. With limited resources and judicious signings, a top-half finish should be a realistic aspiration, however.

Advance Tickets Tel No: 08712 000071
Fax: 020 8771 5311
Ticket Office/Fax: 020 8653 4708
Training Ground: Copers Cope Road, Beckenham BR3 1RJ
Brief History: Founded 1905. Former Grounds: The Crystal Palace (F.A. Cup Finals venue), London County Athletic Ground (Herne Hill), The Nest (Croydon Common Athletic Ground), moved to Selhurst Park in 1924. Founder members 3rd Division (1920). Record attendance 51,482
(Total) Current Capacity: 26,309 (all seated)
Visiting Supporters' Allocation: Approx 2,000 in Arthur Wait Stand
Nearest Railway Station: Selhurst, Norwood Junction and Thornton Heath
Parking (Car): Street parking and Sainsbury's car park
Parking (Coach/Bus): Thornton Heath
Police Force and Tel No: Metropolitan (020 8653 8568)
Disabled Visitors' Facilities:
Wheelchairs: 56 spaces in Arthur Wait and Holmesdale Stands
Blind: Commentary available
Anticipated Development(s): Although the club had plans to reconstruct the Main Stand – indeed had Planning Permission for the work – local opposition has meant that no work has been undertaken. Serious thought is now being given to relocation. The long-running split between ownership of the ground and ownership of the club was resolved in October 2006 when Simon Jordan acquired the freehold of Selhurst Park from Ron Noades for £12 million.

C Club Offices
S Club Shop
E Entrance(s) for visiting supporters
T Toilets for visiting supporters

1 Whitehorse Lane
2 Park Road
3 Arthur Wait Stand
4 Selhurst BR Station (½ mile)
5 Norwood Junction BR Station (¼ mile)
6 Thornton Heath BR Station (½ mile)
7 Car Park (Sainsbury's)

↑ North direction (approx)

◄ 701550
▼ 701566

dagenham and redbridge

London Borough of Barking & Dagenham Stadium, Victoria Road, Dagenham, Essex, RM10 7XL

website: **WWW.DAGGERS.CO.UK**
e:mail: **INFO@DAGGERS.CO.UK**
tel no: **020 8592 1549**
colours: **RED AND WHITE SHIRTS, RED SHORTS**
nickname: **THE DAGGERS**
season 2009/10: **LEAGUE TWO**

Last Season: **8th** (p**46**; w**19**; d**11**; l**16**; gf**77**; ga**53**)

So near and yet so far: in the Daggers' third season in the Football league, John Still's Dagenham & Redbridge team came within a whisker of sneaking into the Play-Offs. In the top half League two for the bulk of the campaign, it looked as though the gap between the team and the top eight – a group that seemed to be pulling away from the rest of the division by March – was insurmountable but a combination of good results for the Daggers – including home wins over eventual champions Brentford and Play-Off chasing Bradford City – saw the Daggers occupying the final Play-Off berth after the 3-0 win away at Notts County. The final crunch game was at home against Shrewsbury Town, the only team that could pip the Daggers for the all-important seventh place. Draw or win and the Daggers were in the Play-Offs; lose and Shrewsbury would snatch seventh – and Shrewsbury had one of the worst away records in the League up until that point with only two wins and 12 draws. Ironically, however, the Shrews took a 2-0 half-time lead and, although the Daggers pulled one back in the second half and had opportunities to snatch the equaliser, the Shrews held out to consign Dagenham to another season in League Two. Potentially, given the progress made over the past few years, Still's team should again have the opportunity for a strong top-half finish in 2009/10.

Advance Tickets Tel No: 020 8592 1549
Fax: 020 8593 7227
Training Ground: Details omitted at Club's request
Brief History: The club has roots in four earlier clubs: Ilford (1881); Leytonstone (1886); Walthamstow Avenue (1900); and Dagenham (1949). Ilford and Leytonstone merged in 1979 and, in 1988, became Redbridge Forest following the incorporation of Walthamstow Athletic. Redbridge Forest moved to Victoria Road in 1991 and formed Dagenham & Redbridge with Dagenham in 1992. Promoted to the Football League at the end of the 2006/07 season. Record attendance (at the Victoria Ground): 7,200; (as Dagenham & Redbridge): 5,949
(Total) Current Capacity: 6,078
Visiting Supporters' Allocation: 1,200 (Pondfield Road End open terrace; all standing) plus 200 seats in Barking College Stand
Nearest Railway Station: Dagenham East (District Line)
Parking (Car): car park at ground or on-street
Parking (Coach/Bus): As directed
Police Force and Tel No: Metropolitan (0300 123 1212)
Disabled Visitors' Facilities:
Wheelchairs: 10 spaces at Pondfield End of Main Stand
Blind: No specific facility
Anticipated Development(s):

CARLING STAND

BARKING COLLEGE STAND
AWAY

PITCH SIZE
112 X 72 yards

BURY ROAD END
(OPEN TERRACE)

PONDFIELD ROAD END
AWAY
(OPEN TERRACE)

NORTH STAND

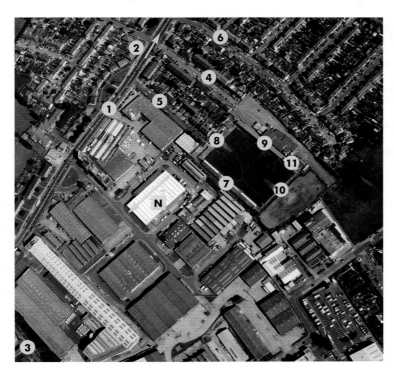

1 A1112 North Rainham Road
2 Dagenham East railway station
3 Oxlow Lane
4 Victoria Road
5 Bury Road
6 Victoria Road
7 North Stand
8 Bury Road Stand
9 Carling Stand
10 Pondfield Road End (away)
11 Family Stand

↑ North direction (approx)

◄ 700788
▼ 700790

darlington

Northern Echo Darlington Arena, Neasham Road, Darlington, DL2 1DL

website: **WWW.DARLINGTON-FC.NET**
e:mail: **RECEPTION@DARLINGTON-FC.NET**
tel no: **01325 387000**
colours: **WHITE AND BLACK SHIRTS, BLACK SHORTS**
nickname: **THE QUAKERS**
season 2009/10: **LEAGUE TWO**

Last Season*: **12th** (p**46**; w**20**; d**12**; l**14**; gf**61**; ga**44**;

Under Derek Penney and with one of the larger budgets in League Two, Darlington's ambitions for the 2008/09 season were clear. However, although always in the chase for a place in the Play-Offs at the very least – indeed when the club lost 1-0 away at non-league Droylsden in the First Round of the FA Cup the Quakers were top of League Two – the wheels came off the team's financial chariot when the club entered Administration. Although the team's performances on the field remained resilient, the automatic 10-point deduction meant that the club's chances of even the Play-Offs were ended. Away from the League, the team achieved a notable 2-1 victory away at League One outfit Walsall in the First Round of the Carling Cup. Towards the end of April it was announced that Penney was leaving to take the helm at League One Oldham; assistant Martin Gray took charge for the final game of the season. Penney leaves the club still in Administration and his successor, the experienced Colin Todd, will face the unenviable task of trying to rebuild a squad on a much-reduced budget capable of competing at this level. Given the circumstances, it's hard to escape the conclusion that 2009/10 could well be a season of toil both on and off the field for Darlington.

Advance Tickets Tel No: 0871 855 1883
Fax: 01325 387050
Training Ground: Details omitted at Club's request
Brief History: Founded 1883. Founder members of 3rd Division (North) 1921. Relegated from 4th Division 1989. Promoted from GM Vauxhall Conference in 1990. Previous Ground: Feethams; moving to Neasham Road in 2003. Record attendance (at Feethams) 21,023; (at Neasham Road) 11,600
(Total) Current Capacity: 25,000
Visiting Supporters' Allocation: 3,000 in East Stand
Nearest Railway Station: Darlington Bank Top
Parking (Car): Spaces available in adjacent car park (£5.00 fee)
Parking (Coach/Bus): As directed
Police Force and Tel No: Durham (01235 467681)
Disabled Visitors Facilities:
Wheelchairs: 165 places
Blind: No special facility
Anticipated Developments: With the construction of the new ground, there are no further plans for development as the existing ground's capacity is more than adequate for League Two.

*10 points deducted as a result of going into Administration in 2009

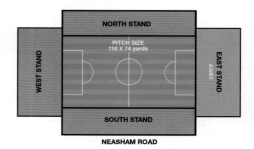

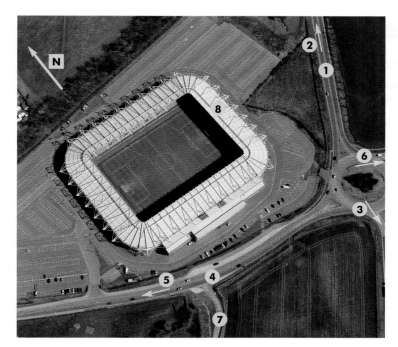

1 A66
2 To Stockton
3 To A66(M) and A1(M)
4 Neasham Road
5 To Darlington town centre
and railway station
(one mile)
6 To Neasham
7 Snipe Lane
8 East Stand (away)

⬆ North direction (approx)

◄ 700522
▼ 700532

derby county

Pride Park, Derby, Derbyshire, DE24 8XL

website: **WWW.DCFC.PREMIUMTV.CO.UK**
e:mail: **DERBY.COUNTY@DCFC.CO.UK**
tel no: **0871 472 1884**
colours: **WHITE SHIRTS, BLACK SHORTS**
nickname: **THE RAMS**
season 2009/10: **CHAMPIONSHIP**

Last Season: **18th** (p**46**; w**14**; d**12**; l**20**; gf**55**; ga**67**)

Relegated at the end of the 2007/08 season from the Premier League, Paul Jewell's Derby County seemed to be making a serious bid for back-to-back relegations as the dire form of the 2007/08 season was replicated in the early months of the new season. It was not until the fifth League match of the season that the Rams registered their first win. With the club struggling – it had been briefly bottom of the division – Jewell departed from the Pride Park hot seat in late December with the club sitting in 18th place. His assistant Chris Hutchings took over as caretaker before the appointment, in early January, of Nigel Clough as the new manager. Clough, who had been manager at non-League Burton Albion for 10 years and had guided the team towards promotion to the League for the first time, stabilised the team and ensured that Championship football will again be on offer at Pride park in 2009/10. As a manager, however, he is untested at this level and the challenges that he and the squad face in maximising the potential from the second and last parachute payment following relegation from the Premier League. County ought to have the potential to reach the Play-Offs but a top-half position is perhaps the most likely result.

Advance Tickets Tel No: 0871 472 1884
Fax: 01332 667540
Training Ground: Moor Farm Training Centre, Morley Road, Oakwood, Derby DE21 4TB
Brief History: Founded 1884. Former grounds: The Racecourse Ground, the Baseball Ground (1894-1997), moved to Pride Park 1997. Founder members of the Football League (1888). Record capacity at the Baseball Ground: 41,826; at Pride Park: 33,597
(Total) Current Capacity: 33,597
Visiting Supporters' Allocation: 5,600 maximum in the South (Winfield Construction) Stand
Nearest Railway Station: Derby
Parking (Car): 2,300 places at the ground designated for season ticket holders. Also two 1,000 car parks on the A6/A52 link road. No on-street parking
Parking (Coach/Bus): As directed
Police Force and Tel No: Derbyshire (01332 290100)
Disabled Visitors' Facilities:
Wheelchairs: 70 home/30 away spaces
Blind: Commentary available
Anticipated Development(s): Although formal proposals have yet to be lodged with the planning authorities, the club is planning a £20 million scheme for a hotel, shops and offices adjacent to Pride Park. There are also plans for the expansion of the ground's capacity to 44,000 via the construction of second tiers on the East, North and South stands. There is however, no time-scale for the work.

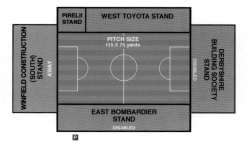

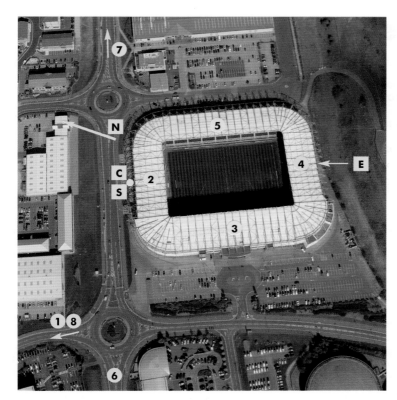

C Club Offices
S Club Shop
E Entrance(s) for visiting
   supporters

1 To Derby Midland BR station
2 North Stand
3 Toyota West Stand
4 South (Cawarden) Stand
   (away)
5 Bombardier East Stand
6 Derwent Parade
7 To A52/M1
8 To City Centre and A6

⬆ *North direction (approx)*

◄ 700534
▼ 700544

doncaster rovers

Keepmoat Stadium, Stadium Way, Lakeside, Doncaster DN4 5JW

website: **WWW.DONCASTERROVERSFC.CO.UK**
e:mail: **INFO@DONCASTERROVERSFC.CO.UK**
tel no: **01302 764664**
colours: **RED AND WHITE SHIRTS, RED SHORTS**
nickname: **THE ROVERS**
season 2009/10: **LEAGUE ONE**

Last Season: **14th** (p**46**; w**17**; d**7**; l**22**; gf**42**; ga**53**)

Promoted via the Play-Offs at the end of the 2007/08 season, it was always likely that Sean O'Driscoll's Rovers would struggle to make an impact in the Championship and for much of the campaign it did look as though Rovers were going to make an immediate return to League One. Hovering in or just above the drop zone for much of the early part of the season, it was not until February and early March when a series of six wins in eight matches lifted the team to the then dizzy heights of 13th did it look as though the team would survive. However, a run of four straight League defeats dropped the team right back into the relegation battle but a late season return to form saw Rovers survive in the Championship in some comfort. Having survived in 2008/09 the club, provided that it can keep key players like Paul Heffernan, should again retain its Championship status in 2009/10 although, as with Colchester United a couple of seasons ago, it could prove once again to be a struggle, particularly as the teams being promoted from League One at the end of the 2008/09 season look stronger than usual.

Advance Tickets Tel No: 01302 762576
Fax: 01302 363525
Training Ground: Cantley Park, Aintree Avenue, Doncaster DN4 6HR
Brief History: Founded 1879. Former grounds: Town Moor, Belle Vue (not later ground), Deaf School Playing Field (later name Intake Ground), Bennetthorpe, Belle Vue (1922-2006). Returned to Football League after a five-year absence in 2003. Record attendance (at Belle Vue) 37,149; (at Keepmoat Stadium) 15,001
(Total) Current Capacity: 15,231
Visiting Supporters' Allocation: 3,350 (North Stand)
Nearest Railway Station: Doncaster (two miles)
Parking (Car): 1,000 place car park at ground
Parking (Coach/Bus): As directed
Other Clubs Sharing Ground: Doncaster Dragons RLFC and Doncaster Belles Ladies FC
Police Force and Tel No: South Yorkshire (01302 366744)
Disabled Visitors' Facilities:
Wheelchairs: Three sides of ground (16-18 at pitch side)
Blind: Commentary available
Anticipated Development(s): The club moved into the new Keepmoat Stadium during the course of the 2006/07 season. The ground, which cost £21 million to construct, is owned by Doncaster Council. There are no plans for further development at this stage.

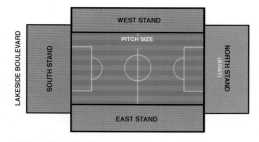

1 Lakeside Boulevard
2 To A6182 White Rose Way
3 To Doncaster town centre and railway station
4 To Junction 3 M18
5 Athletics Stadium
6 Site of 1,000 place car park

⬆ North direction (approx)

◀ 700553
▼ 700550

everton

Goodison Park, Liverpool L4 4EL

website: **WWW.EVERTONFC.COM**
e:mail: **EVERTON@EVERTONFC.COM**
tel no: **0871 663 1878**
colours: **BLUE AND WHITE SHIRTS, WHITE SHORTS**
nickname: **THE TOFFEES**
season 2009/10: **PREMIER LEAGUE**

Last Season: **5th** (p**38**; w**17**; d**12**; l**9**; gf**55**; ga**37**)

Ultimately the best of the rest — the team that finished fifth in the Premier League — Everton's season might have been even better if David Moyes's team hadn't been severely affected by injuries to key players. With one of the smaller squads amongst the division's top teams, to lose players like Yakubu, Jagielka, Jacobsen and Arteta was always going to affect the team's ability to break into the top four. Despite these problems, the Toffees were to reach the FA Cup Final — defeating Liverpool and Manchester United en route — where the club faced Chelsea. It looked as though fortune was going to favour Everton as the club swept into an immediate lead, scoring the fastest ever FA Cup Final goal. However, Chelsea proved too strong, equalising prior to half time before dominating the second half and eventually winning 2-1. For Everton European football, courtesy of the Europa League, beckons in 2009/10 but domestically it's hard to escape the conclusion that, for the team to break into the top-four places, either the squad will need considerable strengthening or one of the existing quartet will need to have a dire campaign. In League terms, fifth is perhaps again the best that can be hoped for with the best hope for silverware perhaps once more via one of the cup competitions.

Advance Tickets Tel No: 0871 663 1878
Fax: 0151 286 9112
Training Ground: Bellefield Training Ground, Sandforth Road, West Derby, Liverpool L12 1LW
Tel: 0151 330 2278
Fax: 0151 284 5181
Brief History: Founded 1879 as St. Domingo, changed to Everton in 1880. Former grounds: Stanley Park, Priory Road and Anfield (Liverpool F.C. ground), moved to Goodison Park in 1892. Founder-members Football League (1888). Record attendance 78,299
(Total) Current Capacity: 40,569 (all seated)
Visiting Supporters' Allocation: 3,000 (part of Bullens Road Stand) maximum
Nearest Railway Station: Kirkdale
Parking (Car): Corner of Utting Avenue and Priory Road
Parking (Coach/Bus): Priory Road
Police Force and Tel No: Merseyside (0151 709 6010)
Disabled Visitors' Facilities:
Wheelchairs: Bullens Road Stand
Blind: Commentary available
Anticipated Development(s): Although Planning Permission for the new ground was granted in June 2008, it was subsequently announced that the project had been called in by the government and that the scheme would be subject to a public enquiry. This started on 18 November 2008 and ended in February 2009; the final decision was due in June 2009. Despite the delays, the club remains committed to the £400 million project, which will see a new 50,000-seat ground constructed in Knowsley.

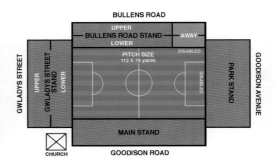

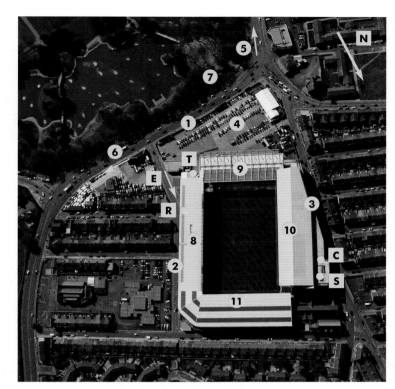

C Club Offices
S Club Shop
E Entrance(s) for visiting supporters
R Refreshment bars for visiting supporters
T Toilets for visiting supporters

1 A580 Walton Road
2 Bullen Road
3 Goodison Road
4 Car Park
5 Liverpool Lime Street BR Station (2 miles)
6 To M57 Junction 2, 4 and 5
7 Stanley Park
8 Bullens Road Stand
9 Park Stand
10 Main Stand
11 Gwladys Stand

↑ North direction (approx)

◄ 702072
▼ 702042

exeter city

St James Park, Stadium Way, Exeter, EX4 6PX

website: **WWW.EXETERCITYFC.CO.UK**
e:mail: **RECEPTION@EXETERCITYFC.CO.UK**
tel no: **01392 411243**
colours: **RED AND WHITE SHIRTS, BLACK SHORTS**
nickname: **THE GRECIANS**
season 2009/10: **LEAGUE ONE**

Last Season: **2nd** (promoted) (p**46**; w**22**; d**13**; l**11**; gf**65**; ga**50**)

Promoted via the Play-Offs from the Blue Square Premier League at the end of the 2007/08 season, Paul Tisdale's Exeter City team proved itself to be the dark horse of the League Two season. Although starting the campaign slowly, once the Grecians had established themselves at this level, the team started an almost inexorable rise up to the table towards both the Play-Offs and ultimately automatic promotion. One of three teams – the others being Bury and Wycombe Wanderers – vying for the final two automatic promotion places on the final day of the season, Exeter's 1-0 victory away at Rotherham was enough to ensure a second successive promotion irrespective of results elsewhere. Thus City are restored to the third tier of English football for the first time since relegation at the end of the 1993/94 season. Other clubs have suffered from a rapid ascent through the divisions and City are likely to face a battle – as with Hereford in 2008/09 – to survive at the higher level. However, provided that the club gets off to a good start in the new season and thus confidence amongst players and fans remains high, then the team should be able to avoid an immediate return to League Two.

Advance Tickets Tel No: 01392 411423
Fax: 01392 413959
Training Ground: Cat & Fiddle Training ground, Sidmouth Road, Clyst St Mary, Exeter EX5 1DP
Brief History: Founded in 1904 as a result of the amalgamation of St Sidwell United and Exeter United. Founder members of Third Division (1920). Relegated to Conference 2003; League status reclaimed 2008
(Total) Current Capacity: 9,036 (3,806 seated)
Visiting Supporters' Allocation: 1,200 (St James' Road End – open terrace) plus limited seats in Flybe Stand. If limited away support is anticipated, then the Flybe Stand accommodation only is used.
Nearest Railway Station: Exeter St James Park
Parking (Car): National Car Park or council car parks (no on-street parking; residents' only scheme in operation)
Parking (Coach/Bus): Paris Street bus station
Police Force and Tel No: Devon & Cornwall (08452 777444)
Disabled Visitors' Facilities:
Wheelchairs: 40 places in Flybe Stand and Big Bank
Blind: No special facility
Anticipated Development(s):

◄ 701389
▼ 701381

fulham

Craven Cottage, Stevenage Road, Fulham, London SW6 6HH

website: **WWW.FULHAMFC.COM**
e:mail: **ENQUIRIES@FULHAMFC.COM**
tel no: **0870 442 1222**
colours: **WHITE SHIRTS, BLACK SHORTS**
nickname: **THE COTTAGERS**
season 2009/10: **PREMIER LEAGUE**

Last Season: **7th** (p**38**; w**14**; d**11**; l**13**; gf**39**; ga**34**)

Escaping relegation by the skin of the club's teeth at the end of the 2007/08 season, Fulham in 2008/09 were ultimately a completely different proposition under the astute management of Roy Hodgson although the season did start unpromisingly for the team, with the club standing just outside the drop zone at the end of October. At that stage it looked as though the Cottagers would face another of the club's annual battles to avoid the drop. However, the team's form picked up and, by the end of the campaign, the club had gathered enough points to finish in seventh place – the club's highest ever finish in the top flight – and thus bring European football to Craven Cottage courtesy of the Europa League. Not all was positive, however, as the club suffered an embarrassing 1-0 defeat against promotion-chasing Burnley in the Third Round of the Carling Cup. For 2009/10, Hodgson will face the challenge of trying to main the club's position in what may well be a stronger Premier League with the additional distraction of European competition as well. The club ought to have the potential again to finish in the top half of the table but a poor start to the season could see confidence slip and a serious battle to avoid the drop.

Club Offices: Fulham FC Training Ground, Motspur Park, New Malden, Surrey KT3 6PT
Advance Tickets Tel No: 0870 442 1234
Fax: 020 8442 0236
Training Ground: The Academy, Fulham FC, Motspur Park, New Malden, Surrey, KT3 6PT; Tel: 020 8336 7430
Brief History: Founded in 1879 as St. Andrews Fulham, changed name to Fulham in 1898. Former grounds: Star Road, Ranelagh Club, Lillie Road, Eel Brook Common, Purer's Cross, Barn Elms, Half Moon (Wasps Rugby Football Ground), Craven Cottage (from 1894), moved to Loftus Road 2002 and returned to Craven Cottage for start of the 2004/05 season. Record Attendance:
Craven Cottage (49,335)
(Total) Current Capacity: 26,400
Visiting Supporters' Allocation: 3,000 in Putney End
Nearest Railway Station: Putney Bridge (Tube)
Parking (Car): Street parking
Parking(Coach/Bus): Stevenage Road
Police Force and Tel No: Metropolitan (020 7741 6212)
Disabled Visitors' Facilities:
Wheelchairs: Main Stand and Hammersmith End
Blind: No special facility
Anticipated Development(s): It was announced in early October that the club was looking to increase Craven Cottage's capacity by some 4,000 by infilling the corners between the corners of the existing stands.

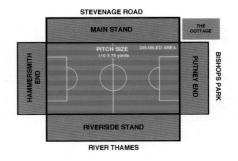

E Entrance(s) for visiting
   supporters
R Refreshment bars for visiting
   supporters
T Toilets for visiting supporters

1 River Thames
2 Stevenage Road
3 Finlay Street
4 Putney Bridge Tube Station
   (0.5 mile)
5 Putney End (away)
6 Riverside Stand
7 Main Stand
8 Hammersmith End
9 Craven Cottage

↑ North direction (approx)

◄ 701570
▼ 701581

gillingham

KRBS Priestfield Stadium, Redfern Avenue, Gillingham, Kent, ME7 4DD

website: **WWW.GILLINGHAMFOOTBALLCLUB.COM**
e:mail: **MEDIA@PRIESTFIELD.COM**
tel no: **01634 300000**
colours: **BLUE AND BLACK HOOPED SHIRTS, BLUE SHORTS**
nickname: **THE GILLS**
season 2009/10: **LEAGUE ONE**

Last Season: **5th** (promoted) (p**46**; w**21**; d**12**; l**13**; gf**68**; ga**55**)

Under Mark Stimson, the Gills ultimately had a successful season, triumphing 1-0 in the League Two Play-Off Final against Shrewsbury Town to gain promotion to League One after only one season at this level following relegation at the end of the 2007/08 season. Never one of the teams vying for automatic promotion, the Gills however, were always in the hunt for one of the Play-Off places and were ultimately to finish in fifth place and thus face a Play-Off Semi-Final against Rochdale. A 0-0 draw at Spotland gave the Gills the edge which the team took advantage of, scoring a 2-1 victory at Priestfield to set up a showdown with Shrewsbury at Wembley. Earlier in the season the Shrews had comprehensively beaten Gillingham 7-0 at the ProStar Stadium and had achieved a 2-2 draw at Priestfield towards the end of the season. Revenge was, therefore, sweet when a last-minute goal settled the Final as the match seemed to be drifting towards extra time. Outside the League, Gillingham also achieved a 2-1 away victory at League One Stockport in the FA Cup Second Round replay. For 2009/10, as a team promoted via the Play-Offs, Gillingham may well struggle to make an impact at the higher level but Stimson ought to be able build a squad capable of ensuring that the team retains its League One status.

Advance Tickets Tel No: 01634 300000
Fax: 01634 850986
Training Ground: Beechings Cross, Grange Road, Gillingham ME7 2UD
Brief History: Founded 1893, as New Brompton, changed name to Gillingham in 1913. Founder-members Third Division (1920). Lost Football League status (1938), re-elected to Third Division South (1950). Record attendance 23,002
(Total) Current Capacity: 11,582 (all seated)
Visiting Supporters' Allocation: 1,500 (in Gillingham (Brian Moore Stand) End)
Nearest Railway Station: Gillingham
Parking (Car): Street parking
Parking (Coach/Bus): As directed by Police
Police Force and Tel No: Kent (01634 234488)
Disabled Visitors' Facilities:
Wheelchairs: Redfern Avenue (Main) Stand
Blind: No special facility
Anticipated Development(s): The old open Town End Terrace was demolished during 2003 and replaced by a new temporary open stand. Planning Permission was granted in 2003 for the construction of a new 3,500-seat stand, to be named after noted fan the late Brian Moore, although work has yet to commence. Despite the investment at Priestfield, however, the club is investigating, in conjunction with the local council, the possibility of constructing a new stadium at Temple Marsh. Towards the end of January 2008, chairman Paul Scally announced that he hoped to make a statement about relocation within six weeks with a view to the club moving to a new site within the Medway area for the start of the 2010/11 season but there has been little to report since then.

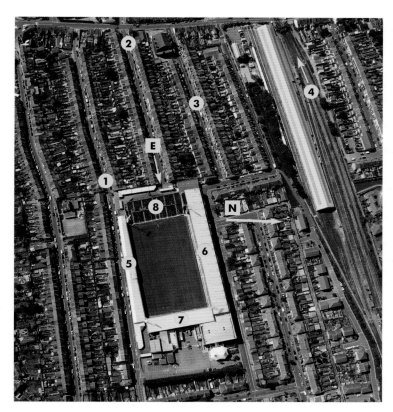

E Entrance(s) for visiting supporters

1 Redfern Avenue
2 Toronto Road
3 Gordon Road
4 Gillingham BR station (¼ mile)
5 Gordon Street Stand
6 New two-tier Main (Medway) Stand
7 New Rainham End Stand
8 Gillingham End; uncovered seating (away)

↑ North direction (approx)

◀ 700771
▼ 700780

grimsby town

Blundell Park, Cleethorpes, DN35 7PY

website: **WWW.GRIMSBY–TOWNFC.PREMIUMTV.CO.UK**
e:mail: **MAILBOX@GTFC.CO.UK**
tel no: **01472 605050**
colours: **BLACK AND WHITE STRIPED SHIRTS, BLACK SHORTS**
nickname: **THE MARINERS**
season 2009/10: **LEAGUE TWO**

Last Season: **22nd** (p**46**; w**9**; d**14**; l**23**; gf**51**; ga**69**)

Following a 3-1 home defeat to lowly Chester City in mid-September, which left the team with only two points from its first six League matches, Alan Buckley was dismissed as manager. In early October the ex-Luton Town boss, the experienced Mike Newell, was brought in as new manager and, in his first game, almost managed to achieve the perfect start against high-flying Wycombe; it took a last-minute equaliser for Wanderers to salvage a draw and deny the Mariners their first victory of the League season. It was not until the club's 16th League match of the season – away at high-flying Bury – that Newell's team finally achieved a League victory and all of that time Bournemouth was slowly whittling away at the 17-point deduction. As the season drew on, it became clear that there was effectively a three-horse race to fill the final relegation place – Luton were always too far adrift to be a serious contender for League survival: Bournemouth, Chester and Grimsby. Of the three, Bournemouth had the playing ability of a mid-table outfit and so, realistically, the drop came down to either Grimsby or Chester. It was the results on the penultimate day of the season that effectively ensured that Grimsby stayed up. Needing a victory at Aldershot to take battle to the wire – Chester's abysmal goal difference meant that they always needed to be ahead of Grimsby on points – the resulting 2-2 draw was enough to ensure that Grimsby lived to fight another day in League Two despite only drawing on the final day. Grimsby only survived in 2008/09 as a result of other clubs' financial misfortunes; it's hard to escape the belief that they'll need to benefit from similar circumstances in 2009/10 if the club is to survive in the League.

Advance Tickets Tel No: 01472 605050
Fax: 01472 693665
Training Ground: Cheapside, Waltham, Grimsby
Brief History: Founded in 1878, as Grimsby Pelham, changed name to Grimsby Town in 1879. Former Grounds: Clee Park (two adjacent fields) and Abbey Park, moved to Blundell Park in 1899. Founder-members 2nd Division (1892). Record attendance 31,651
(Total) Current Capacity: 9,546 (all seated)
Visiting Supporters' Allocation: 2,200 in Osmond Stand
Nearest Railway Station: Cleethorpes
Parking (Car): Street parking
Parking (Coach/Bus): Harrington Street
Police Force and Tel No: Humberside (01472 359171)
Disabled Visitors' Facilities:
Wheelchairs: Harrington Street (Main) Stand
Blind: Commentary available
Anticipated Development(s): In late January 2006 it was announced that the club had applied for planning permission to construct a new 20,100-seat ground, to be called the ConocoPhillips Stadium, at Great Coates. Outline planning permission for the work was granted in early 2007. The cost, some £14.4 million, includes a £10 million retail park, with the first phase providing a 12,000-seat facility. Planning permission was granted in December 2007.

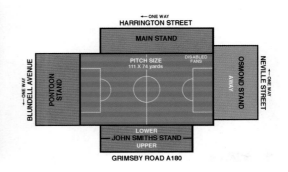

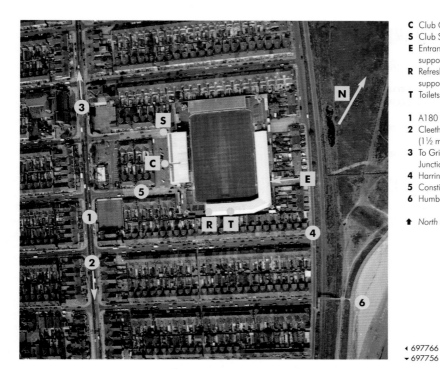

C Club Offices
S Club Shop
E Entrance(s) for visiting
supporters
R Refreshment bars for visiting
supporters
T Toilets for visiting supporters

1 A180 Grimsby Road
2 Cleethorpes BR Station
(1½ miles)
3 To Grimsby and M180
Junction 5
4 Harrington Street
5 Constitutional Avenue
6 Humber Estuary

↑ *North direction (approx)*

◀ 697766
▼ 697756

hartlepool united

Victoria Park, Clarence Road, Hartlepool, TS24 8BZ

website: **WWW.HARTLEPOOLUNITED.CO.UK**
e:mail: **ENQUIRIES@HARTLEPOOLUNITED.CO.UK**
tel no: **01429 272584**
colours: **BLUE AND WHITE STRIPED SHIRTS, BLUE SHORTS**
nickname: **THE POOLS**
season 2009/10: **LEAGUE ONE**

Last Season: **19th** (p**46**; w**13**; d**11**; l**22**; gf**66**; ga**79**)

In mid-December, following a 1-1 draw away at struggling Hereford United, a result that left United in 13th place in League One, Danny Wilson departed the managerial hot seat after some two-and-a-half years in charge. He was replaced immediately by Chris Turner, the club's Director of Football. Under Turner, the club achieved a notable scalp in the Third Round of the FA Cup, defeating Premier League Stoke City at home 2-0, but struggled in the League. Mathematically, United was one of five clubs that might have faced last-day relegation, and a 4-1 defeat at Bristol Rovers could have been worse if results elsewhere had gone against the team. If Northampton had managed to gain a point at Elland Road or if Carlisle had score one more goal at home against Millwall, then it might have been Hartlepool rather than Northampton facing the trip to Burton Albion. For 2009/10, it's hard to escape the conclusion that the club may well face another battle to retain League One status.

Advance Tickets Tel No: 01429 272584
Fax: 01429 863007
Training Ground: Details omitted at club's request
Brief History: Founded 1908 as Hartlepools United, changed to Hartlepool (1968) and to Hartlepool United in 1977. Founder-members 3rd Division (1921). Record attendance 17,426
(Total) Current Capacity: 7,787 (4,180 seated)
Visiting Supporters' Allocation: 1,000 (located in Rink Stand)
Nearest Railway Station: Hartlepool Church Street
Parking (Car): Street parking and rear of clock garage
Parking (Coach/Bus): As directed
Police Force and Tel No: Cleveland (01429 221151)
Disabled Visitors' Facilities:
Wheelchairs: Cyril Knowles Stand and Rink End
Blind: Commentary available
Anticipated Development(s): The plans for the redevelopment of the Millhouse Stand are still progressing, although there is now no definite timescale. When this work does commence, the ground's capacity will be reduced to 5,000 temporarily.

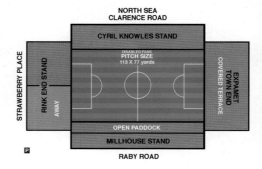

C Club Offices
S Club Shop
E Entrance(s) for visiting
supporters

1 A179 Clarence Road
2 To Hartlepool Church Street
BR Station
3 To Marina Way
4 Site of former Greyhound
Stadium
5 To Middlesbrough A689 &
A1(M)
6 To A19 North
7 Rink End Stand

⬆ *North direction (approx)*

◄ 700556
▼ 700565

hereford united

Edgar Street, Hereford, HR4 9JU

website: **WWW.HEREFORDUNITED.CO.UK**
e:mail: **HUFC1939@HOTMAIL.COM**
tel no: **0844 276 1939**
colours: **WHITE SHIRTS, WHITE SHORTS**
nickname: **THE BULLS**
season 2009/10: **LEAGUE TWO**

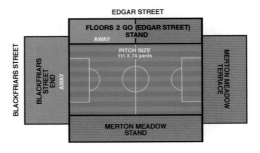

EDGAR STREET

FLOORS 2 GO (EDGAR STREET) STAND
AWAY

PITCH SIZE
111 X 74 yards

BLACKFRIARS STREET

BLACKFRIARS STREET END
AWAY

MERTON MEADOW TERRACE

MERTON MEADOW STAND

Last Season: **24th** (relegated) (p**46**; w**9**; d**7**; l**30**; gf**42**; ga**79**)

A hugely disappointing season for the Bulls after their second promotion in three seasons saw Graham Turner's team return to League Two after only one year at League One level. In the relegation zone for much of the season and having amassed only 17 points after 23 games, the club's relegation was confirmed well before the end of the season following a run of 11 defeats in 12 matches. The club's major problem was up front, where the team managed to score only 42 League goals all year – the second lowest in League One – combined with a leaky defence; the club's negative goal difference was only better than that of Cheltenham, another club that will be joining United in League Two in 2009/10. Following the end of the season it was confirmed that Turner had stood down as manager – he remains as club chairman – to be replaced as boss by first-team coach John Trewick. With a number of highly ambitious teams having been promoted from League Two at the end of 2008/09 and with the remaining clubs facing increasing financial stringency, the lower division looks very open and United, as a relegated team, ought to have the pedigree to make a serious bid for the Play-Offs at the very least.

Advance Tickets Tel No: 0844 276 1939
Fax: 01432 341359
Training Ground: details omitted at club's request
Brief History: Founded 1924; first elected to the Football League 1972; relegated to the Conference 1997; promoted through the Play-Offs at the end of 2005/06. Record attendance 18,115
(Capacity 5,300; 2,761 seated)
Visiting Supporters' Allocation: tbc
Nearest Railway Station: Hereford
Parking (Car): Merton Meadow and Edgar Street
Parking (Coach/Bus): Cattle Market
Police Force and Tel No: West Mercia (08457 444888)
Disabled Visitors' Facilities:
Wheelchairs: Edgar Street (limited)
Blind: Commentary available
Anticipated Development(s): After some years of deterioration, the Blackfriars Street End was finally closed during the summer of 2009 and this has resulted in the reduction to 5,300 in the ground's total capacity.
On 15 July 2009 the club announced its intention to construct a new 2,000-capacity covered terrace at this end. There is no confirmed timescale for the work.

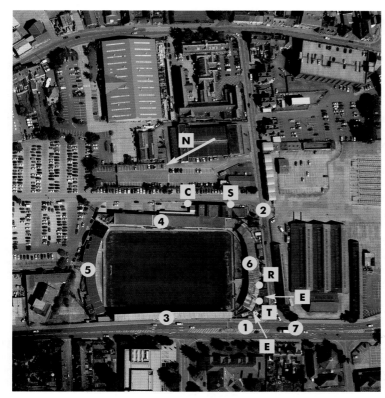

C Club Offices
S Club Shop
E Entrance(s) for visiting
   supporters
R Refreshment bars for visiting
   supporters
T Toilets for visiting supporters

1 A49(T) Edgar Street
2 Blackfriars Street
3 Edgar Street Stand
4 Merton Meadow Stand
5 Merton Meadow Terrace
6 Blackfriars Street End
7 To Town Centre and
   Hereford BR Station

↑ *North direction (approx)*

◄ 700427
▼ 700436

huddersfield town

The Galpharm Stadium, Leeds Road, Huddersfield, HD1 6PX

website: **WWW.HTAFC.COM**
e:mail: **INFO@HTAFC.COM**
tel no: **0870 444 4677**
colours: **BLUE AND WHITE STRIPED SHIRTS, WHITE SHORTS**
nickname: **THE TERRIERS**
season 2009/10: **LEAGUE ONE**

Last Season: **9th** (p**46**; w**18**; d**14**; l**14**; gf**62**; ga**65**)

Although only appointed in the summer, Stan Ternent's tenancy of the managerial seat at the Galpharm Stadium was destined to be short-lived, as he departed in early November following a 3-2 victory over Crewe Alexandra that left the Terriers in 16th place in League One. In Ternent's 15 matches in charge the club had only won four. Gerry Murphy was again appointed as caretaker – a role he had also assumed during the previous season when Andy Ritchie departed – along with Graham Mitchell before the appointment of Lee Clark, the ex-Newcastle, Fulham and Sunderland player, as new manager in early December. Clark, in his first managerial role, guided Town up the League One table, ultimately reaching a creditable ninth place. Although the Play-Offs were always going to be out of reach, given the early season form, provided that the progress on the field seen in the second half of the 2008/09 season is maintained in 2009/10, the club ought to be one of those pushing for a Play-Off place at the very least.

Advance Tickets Tel No: 0870 444 4552
Fax: 01484 484101
Training Ground: Storthes Hall, Storthes Hall Lane, Kirkburton, Huddersfield HD8 0WA
Brief History: Founded 1908, elected to Football League in 1910. First Club to win the Football League Championship three years in succession. Moved from Leeds Road ground to Kirklees (Alfred McAlpine) Stadium 1994/95 season. Record attendance (Leeds Road) 67,037; Galpharm Stadium: 23,678
(Total) Current Capacity: 24,500 (all seated)
Visiting Supporters' Allocation: 4,037 (all seated)
Nearest Railway Station: Huddersfield
Parking (Car): Car parks (pre-sold) adjacent to ground
Parking (Coach/Bus): Car parks adjacent to ground
Other Clubs Sharing Ground: Huddersfield Giants RLFC
Police Force and Tel No: West Yorkshire (01484 422122)
Disabled Visitors' Facilities:
Wheelchairs: Three sides of Ground, at low levels and raised area, including toilet access
Blind: Area for partially sighted with Hospital Radio commentary
Anticipated Development(s): With completion of the new North Stand, work on the Galpharm Stadium is over.

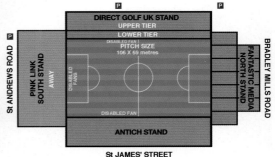

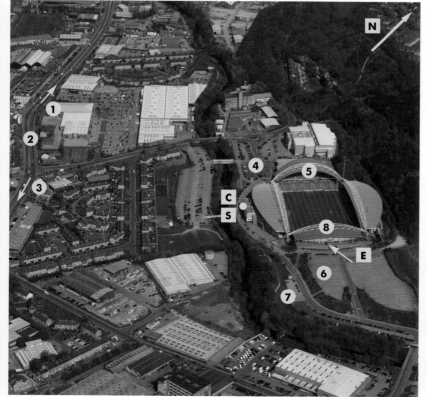

N

C Club Offices
S Club Shop
E Entrance(s) for visiting supporters

1 To Leeds and M62 Junction 25
2 A62 Leeds Road
3 To Huddersfield BR station (1¼ miles)
4 Disabled parking
5 North Stand
6 St Andrews pay car park
7 Coach park
8 South (Pink Link) Stand (away)

↑ North direction (approx)

hull city

Kingston Communications Stadium, Walton Street, Hull, East Yorkshire, HU3 6HU

website: **WWW.HULLCITYAFC.NET**
e:mail: **INFO@HULLTIGERS.COM**
tel no: **0870 837 0003**
colours: **AMBER SHIRTS, BLACK SHORTS**
nickname: **THE TIGERS**
season 2009/10: **PREMIER LEAGUE**

Last Season: **17th** (p**38**; w**8**; d**11**; l**19**; gf**39**; ga**64**)

Promoted at the end of the 2007/08 season, Hull City went from heroes to near zeroes in the space of a single season. Although football is widely seen as a game of two halves, few teams have explored this theme as thoroughly as the Tigers over the course of a single season. Widely regarded as automatic candidates for an immediate return to the Championship, Phil Brown's team arrived in the Premier League as a breath of fresh air and took the first half of the season by storm, standing in fifth position in early December with 26 points from 16 League matches and a number of notable scalps – most notably Arsenal at the Emirates Stadium – under the belt. The last 22 League matches, however, brought but one victory and 16 defeats as the team plummeted down the Premier League table with the serious threat of relegation not being lifted until the final day of the season. One of four teams that could have joined West Brom back in the Championship had results gone against them, the Tigers faced the grim prospect of a home match against Manchester United. Although United won 1-0, results elsewhere, most notably Newcastle's defeat at Aston Villa, meant that the Tigers survived. A number of other teams have suffered in their second season at this level and it's hard to escape the conclusion that Brown's team will again face an uphill battle to survive and relegation must be a very serious possibility.

Advance Tickets Tel No: 0870 837 0004
Fax: 01482 304882
Training Ground: Millhouse Woods Lane, Cottingham, Kingston upon Hull HU16 4HB
Brief History: Founded 1904. Former grounds: The Boulevard (Hull Rugby League Ground), Dairycoates, Anlaby Road Cricket Circle (Hull Cricket Ground), Anlaby Road, Boothferry Park (from 1946). Moved to Kingston Communications Stadium in late 2002. Record attendance (at Boothferry Park) 55,019; (at Kingston Communications Stadium) 25,280
(Total) Current Capacity: 25,504 (all seated)
Visiting Supporters' Allocation: 2,500 all-seated in North Stand
Nearest Railway Station: Hull Paragon
Parking (Car): There are 1,800 spaces on the Walton Street Fairground for use on match days
Parking (Coach/Bus): As directed
Other Clubs Sharing Ground: Hull RLFC
Police Force and Tel No: Humberside (01482 220148)
Disabled Visitors' facilities:
Wheelchairs: c300 places
Blind: Contact club for details
Anticipated Development(s): The club moved into the new Kingston Communication Stadium towards the end of 2002. The ground is shared with Hull RLFC. The total cost of the 25,504-seat ground was £44million. The West Stand is provided with two tiers and there are plans for the construction of a second tier on the East and South Stands, taking the capacity to 34,000, if required.

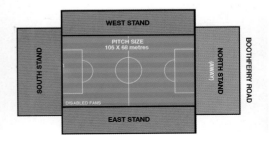

1 A1105 Anlaby Road
2 Arnold Lane
3 West Stand
4 East Stand
5 Walton Street
6 To city centre and railway
   station
7 Car parks
8 Railway line towards
   Scarborough
9 Railway line towards Leeds
10 A1105 westwards towards
   A63 and M62

↑ *North direction (approx)*

◄ 700568
▼ 700578

ipswich town

Portman Road, Ipswich, IP1 2DA

website: **WWW.ITFC.CO.UK**
e:mail: **ENQUIRIES@ITFC.CO.UK**
tel no: **01473 400500**
colours: **BLUE SHIRTS, WHITE SHORTS**
nickname: **THE TRACTORBOYS**
season 2009/10: **CHAMPIONSHIP**

Last Season: **9th** (p**46**; w**17**; d**15**; l**14**; gf**62**; ga**53**)

At the start of the 2008/09 season much was expected of the Tractor Boys as manager Jim Magilton had been given a multi-million war chest by new owner Marcus Evans to fund a sustained push towards automatic promotion or the Play-Offs. In the event, Town's season never really caught fire and the club ended up as one of the also-rans in the chase for the final Play-Off place. As the season wore on it became increasingly clear that Magilton, who had been manager at Portman Road since 2006, was losing the trust of the supporters and it came as no surprise that, in late April with the Play-Offs already non-achievable, he paid the price for the team's failure. The club moved swiftly to appoint the ex-Sunderland manager Roy Keane to the post. With an ambitious chairman allied to a high-profile manager, Town will undoubtedly start as again one of the favourites for the Play-Offs at least. In an otherwise unsatisfactory season, one highpoint was the home victory over Norwich City – ironically Magilton's last game in charge – which helped to consign the Canaries to relegation to League One.

Advance Tickets Tel No: 0870 1110555

Fax: 01473 400040

Training Ground: Ipswich Town Academy, Playford Road, Rushmere, Ipswich IP4 5RU

Brief History: Founded 1887 as Ipswich Association F.C., changed to Ipswich Town in 1888. Former Grounds: Broom Hill & Brookes Hall, moved to Portman Road in 1888. Record attendance 38,010

(Total) Current Capacity: 30,311 (all seated)

Visiting Supporters' Allocation: 1,900 all seated in Cobbold Stand

Nearest Railway Station: Ipswich

Parking (Car): Portman Road, Portman Walk & West End Road

Parking (Coach/Bus): West End Road

Police Force and Tel No: Suffolk (01473 611611)

Disabled Visitors' Facilities:

Wheelchairs: Lower Britannia Stand

Blind: Commentary available

Anticipated Development(s): The new Greene King (South) Stand has been followed by the construction of the new two-tier, 7,035-seat, North Stand, which was initially delayed as a result of legal action. The completion of the two stands takes Portman Road's capacity to more than 30,000.

C Club Offices
E Entrance(s) for visiting supporters
R Refreshment bars for visiting supporters
T Toilets for visiting supporters

1 A137 West End Road
2 Sir Alf Ramsay Way
3 Portman Road
4 Princes Street
5 To Ipswich BR Station
6 Car Parks
7 Cobbold Stand
8 Britannia Stand
9 North Stand
10 Greene King (South) Stand

↑ North direction (approx)

◄ 699778
▼ 699784

leeds united

Elland Road, Leeds, LS11 0ES

website: **WWW.LEEDSUNITED.COM**
e:mail: **RECEPTION@LEEDSUNITED.COM**
tel no: **0871 334 1919**
colours: **WHITE SHIRTS, WHITE SHORTS**
nickname: **THE WHITES**
season 2009/10: **LEAGUE ONE**

Last Season: **4th** (p**46**; w**26**; d**6**; l**14**; gf**77**; ga**49**)

Having lost out in the Play-Off final at the end of the 2007/08 season, hopes were high at Elland Road that the new season would see United once again push for automatic promotion and, without the handicap of the points deduction that had hampered the previous year's season, many pundits agreed. However, a run of four League defeats and an embarrassing 1-0 defeat away at non-League Histon in the Second Round of the FA Cup led to the departure of Gary McAllister as manager just before Christmas with the team standing in ninth place outside the Play-Off places. The club moved quickly to appoint Simon Grayson, then the manager at Blackpool, to the vacant position and under Grayson a Play-Off place was secured. In the Play-Offs, United faced Millwall and a 1-0 victory for the Londoners at home gave Millwall the edge and, despite playing in front of the largest crowd outside the Premier League in the 2008/09 season, a 1-1 draw was insufficient to take United back to Wembley. Thus United face a third season in League One; again the team will be one of the favourites for promotion but with potentially strong teams being relegated from the Championship, the team's route back to English football's second tier may have to be via the Play-Offs.

Advance Tickets Tel No: 0871 334 1992
Fax: 0113 367 6050
Training Ground: Thorp Arch, Walton Road, Nr Wetherby LS23 7BA
Brief History: Founded 1919, formed from the former 'Leeds City' club, who were disbanded following expulsion from the Football League in October 1919. Joined Football League in 1920. Record attendance 57,892
(Total) Current Capacity: 40,296 all seated)
Visiting Supporters' Allocation: 1,800 in South East Corner (can be increased to 5,000 in South Stand if necessary)
Nearest Railway Station: Leeds City
Parking (Car): Car parks adjacent to ground
Parking (Coach/Bus): As directed by Police
Police Force and Tel No: West Yorkshire (0113 243 5353)
Disabled Visitors' Facilities:
Wheelchairs: West Stand and South Stand
Blind: Commentary available
Anticipated Development(s): The club announced plans in late 2008 for the construction of a hotel and other facilities behind the East Stand although there is no timescale for the work at present.

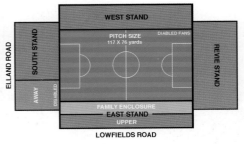

C Club Offices
S Club Shop

1 M621
2 M621 Junction 2
3 A643 Elland Road
4 Lowfields Road
5 To A58
6 To City Centre and
   BR station
7 To M62 and M1

⬆ *North direction (approx)*

◀ 702251
▼ 702259

leicester city

Walkers Stadium, Filbert Road, Leicester, LE2 7FL

website: **WWW.LCFC.COM**
e:mail: **TICKET.SALES@LCFC.CO.UK**
tel no: **0844 815 6000**
colours: **BLUE SHIRTS, WHITE SHORTS**
nickname: **THE FOXES**
season 2009/10: **CHAMPIONSHIP**

Last Season: **1st** (Promoted) (p**46**; w**27**; d**15**; l**4**; gf**84**; ga**39**)

Relegated at the end of the 2007/08 season to League One, Nigel Pearson's Leicester City side was always going to be one of the favourites for automatic promotion and, in this, the Foxes did not disappoint. In the promotion hunt for the entire campaign, the team was to achieve both promotion and the League One title well before the end of the season. As a promoted team, it may well take City a period to adjust to playing at the higher level but the club certainly has the pedigree and the experience to survive in the Championship although, as with teams such as Nottingham Forest, it may prove to be a struggle. A season of consolidation perhaps beckons with a mid-table position being perhaps the reward. Although not dominant, the early season form was encouraging, with the team in or around the top-two spots for the bulk of the campaign.

Advance Tickets Tel No: 0844 815 5000
Fax: 0116 247 0585
Training Ground: Middlesex Road, Leicester LE2 8PB
Brief History: Founded 1884 as Leicester Fosse, changed name to Leicester City in 1919. Former grounds: Fosse Road South, Victoria Road, Belgrave Cycle Track, Mill Lane, Aylstone Road Cricket Ground and Filbert Street (from 1891). The club moved to the new Walkers Stadium for the start of the 2002/03 season. Record attendance (at Filbert Street) 47,298; (at Walkers Stadium) 32,148
(Total) Current Capacity: 32,500
Visiting Supporters' Allocation: 3,000 (all seated) in North East of ground
Nearest Railway Station: Leicester
Parking (Car): NCP car park
Parking (Coach/Bus): As directed
Police Force and Tel No: Leicester (0116 222 2222)
Disabled Visitors Facilities:
Wheelchairs: 186 spaces spread through all stands
Blind: Match commentary via hospital radio
Anticipated Developments: The club moved into the new 32,500-seat Walkers Stadium at the start of the 2002/03 season. Although there are no plans at present, the stadium design allows for the construction of a second tier to the East Stand, taking capacity to 40,000.

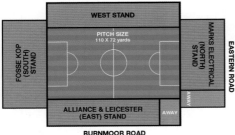

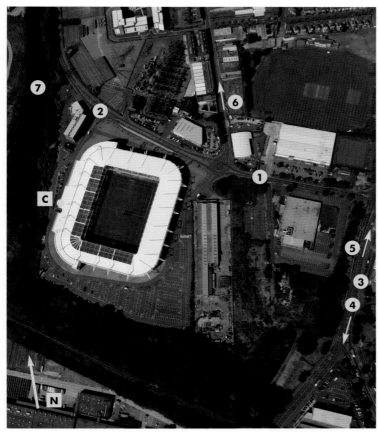

C Club Offices

1 Raw Dykes Road
2 Eastern Road
3 A426 Aylestone Road
4 To Lutterworth
5 To city centre and railway
station (one mile)
6 Burnmoor Street
7 River Soar

⬆ *North direction (approx)*

◀ 702650
▾ 702661

leyton orient

Matchroom Stadium, Brisbane Road, Leyton, London, E10 5NF

website: **WWW.LEYTONORIENT.COM**
e:mail: **INFO@LEYTONORIENT.NET**
tel no: **0871 310 1881**
colours: **RED SHIRTS, RED SHORTS**
nickname: **THE O'S**
season 2009/10: **LEAGUE ONE**

Last Season: **14th** (p**46**; w**15**; d**11**; l**20**; gf**45**; ga**57**)

In mid-January, after more than five years as Orient's manager, Martin Ling departed from the club following the 2-1 defeat by Bristol Rovers and a run that had seen the team endure its fifth successive defeat and its eighth game without a win, leaving Orient in 21st position. Initially Kevin Nugent was appointed caretaker-manager but, in early February, it was announced that ex-Colchester United boss Geraint Williams would take over until the end of the season with Nugent acting as his assistant. Under the new managerial team, Orient gradually moved up the League One table and, at the end of April, it was confirmed that Williams and Nugent would remain in charge for the 2009/10 season. Williams had success with Colchester at this level and his experience should help Orient towards a top-half finish in the new season.

Advance Tickets Tel No: 0871 310 1883

Fax: 0871 310 1882

Training Ground: Southgate Hockey Centre, Trent Park, Snakes Lane, Barnet EN4 0PS

Brief History: Founded 1887 as Clapton Orient, from Eagle Cricket Club (formerly Glyn Cricket Club formed in 1881). Changed name to Leyton Orient (1946), Orient (1966), Leyton Orient (1987). Former grounds: Glyn Road, Whittles Athletic Ground, Millfields Road, Lea Bridge Road, Wembley Stadium (2 games), moved to Brisbane Road in 1937. Record attendance 34,345

(Total) Current Capacity: 9,271 all seated)

Visiting Supporters' Allocation: 1,000 (all seated) in East Stand/Terrace

Nearest Railway Station: Leyton (tube), Leyton Midland Road

Parking (Car): Street parking

Parking (Coach/Bus): As directed by Police

Police Force and Tel No: Metropolitan (020 8556 8855)

Disabled Visitors' Facilities:

Wheelchairs: Windsor Road

Blind: Match commentary supplied on request

Anticipated Development(s): Work was scheduled to start on the North Stand towards the end of October 2006 and the new 1,351-seat structure was completed by the end of the 2006/07 season. In the summer of 2007 plans for the 2012 Olympic Stadium were announced. A permanent capacity of 25,000 is anticipated with a temporary upper tier offering a total capacity of 80,000 for the duration of the Games. There is a possibility, given that no post-2012 use has as yet been identified for the stadium, that Leyton Orient may relocate to the ground for the start of the 2013/14 season.

E Entrance(s) for visiting supporters

1 Buckingham Road
2 Oliver Road
3 A112 High Road Leyton
4 To Leyton Tube Station (¼ mile)
5 Brisbane Road
6 Windsor Road
7 To Leyton Midland Road BR station
8 South Stand
9 West Stand
10 Main (East) Stand
11 North Stand

↑ *North direction (approx)*

◀ 701472
▼ 701477

lincoln city

Sincil Bank, Lincoln LN5 8LD

website: **WWW.REDIMPS.CO.UK**
e:mail: **LCFC@REDIMPS.COM**
tel no: **0870 899 2005**
colours: **RED AND WHITE STRIPES, BLACK SHORTS**
nickname: **THE IMPS**
season 2009/10: **LEAGUE TWO**

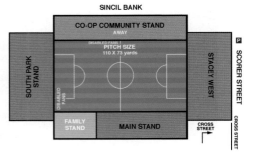

SINCIL BANK

CO-OP COMMUNITY STAND
AWAY

DISABLED FANS
PITCH SIZE
110 X 73 yards

SOUTH PARK STAND

DISABLED FANS

STACEY WEST

P SCORER STREET

FAMILY STAND

MAIN STAND

CROSS STREET

CROSS STREET

Last Season: **13th** (p**46**; w**14**; d**17**; l**15**; gf**53**; ga**52**)

One of the teams that were in the hunt for a Play-Off place for much of the season, the Imps ultimately finished a disappointing 13th place some 10 points adrift of the relatively – and artificially – low total secured by Shrewsbury Town in finishing seventh. At the start of April Peter Jackson's side was only six points adrift with a game in hand but a run of four draws and two defeats in the final six League matches saw the gap grow. Away from the League, the Imps were to suffer an embarrassing 2-1 home defeat by non-League Kettering Town in the First Round of the FA Cup. For 2009/10 Jackson has been told that, like a number of other managers in League Two, he will have to operate on a reduced budget. He is, however, an experienced manager and, given the fact that other teams are in the same boat, this financial burden may not prove insurmountable. The team should again secure a top-half finish with the potential, perhaps, for a Play-Off place.

Advance Tickets Tel No: 0870 899 1976
Fax: 01522 880020
Training Ground: The Sports Ground, Carlton Boulevard, Lincoln LN2 4WJ
Brief History: Founded 1884. Former Ground: John O'Gaunts Ground, moved to Sincil Bank in 1895. Founder-members 2nd Division Football League (1892). Relegated from 4th Division in 1987, promoted from GM Vauxhall Conference in 1988. Record attendance 23,196
(Total) Current Capacity: 10,130 (all seated)
Visiting Supporters' Allocation: 2,000 in Co-op Community Stand (part, remainder for Home fans)
Nearest Railway Station: Lincoln Central
Parking (Car): City centre car parks; limited on-street parking
Parking (Coach/Bus): South Common
Police Force and Tel No: Lincolnshire (01522 529911)
Disabled Visitors' Facilities:
Wheelchairs: The Simons and South (Mundy) Park stands
Blind: No special facility
Anticipated Development(s): Following the replacement of the seats in the Stacey West Stand, Sincil Bank is once again an all-seater stadium.

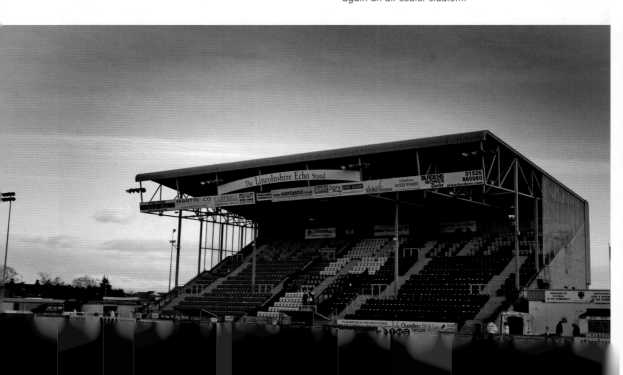

C Club Offices
S Club Shop

1 Family Stand
2 Sincil Bank
3 Sausthorpe Street
4 Cross Street
5 Co-op Community Stand (away)
6 A15 South Park Avenue
7 Stacey West Stand
8 Lincoln Central BR Station (½ mile)

↑ North direction (approx)

◄ 700580
▼ 700587

liverpool

Anfield, Anfield Road, Liverpool L4 0TH

website: **WWW.LIVERPOOLFC.TV**
e:mail: **VIA WEBSITE**
tel no: **0151 263 2361**
colours: **RED SHIRTS, RED SHORTS**
nickname: **THE REDS**
season 2009/10: **PREMIER LEAGUE**

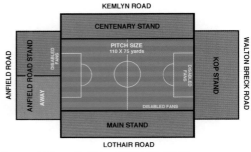

Last Season: **2nd** (p**38**; w**25**; d**11**; l**2**; gf**77**; ga**27**)

Another season of 'what might have been' for Rafael Benitez's Liverpool side saw the team make more of a sustained challenge to Manchester United for the Premier League title – indeed Liverpool doing the double over their main rivals in the middle of March seemed to throw the title race wide open once again – but the reality was that Liverpool was always trying to play catch-up once United's season got fired up. Although Liverpool only lost two matches in the League all season – a record for a club not actually to win the title – the reality was that injuries to key players – most notably Steven Gerrard and Fernando Torres – and an inability to defeat supposedly poorer teams in the League at Anfield – such as Fulham and Stoke – cost Liverpool dear. Away from the League, the club's other main route to silverware – the various cup competitions – failed to bring any success as well, although the team did feature in one of the all-time classic encounters when drawing 4-4 at Stamford Bridge in the Champions League Quarter-Final against Chelsea. Having lost 3-1 at Anfield in the first leg, Liverpool had it all to do in the away match but for much of the second leg it looked as though the Reds were going to defy the odds but the task ultimately proved too difficult. For 2009/10, although Benitez's budget for signings looked constrained, Liverpool should retain the key players from 2008/09 and be able to strengthen the squad; the result ought to be a greater challenge for the title in the new season but, as last year, much may depend upon the fitness of Gerrard and Torres.

Advance Tickets Tel No: 0870 220 2345

Fax: 0151 260 8813

Ticket Enquiries Fax: 0151 261 1416

Training Ground: Melwood Drive, West Derby, Liverpool L12 8SV; Tel: 0151 282 8888

Brief History: Founded 1892. Anfield Ground formerly Everton F.C. Ground. Joined Football League in 1893. Record attendance 61,905

(Total) Current Capacity: 45,362 all seated)

Visiting Supporters' Allocation: 1,972 (all seated) in Anfield Road Stand

Nearest Railway Station: Kirkdale

Parking (Car): Stanley car park

Parking (Coach/Bus): Priory Road and Pinehurst Avenue

Police Force and Tel No: Merseyside (0151 709 6010)

Disabled Visitors' Facilities:

Wheelchairs: Kop and Main Stands

Blind: Commentary available

Anticipated Development(s): Full planning permission was granted in June 2008 for the construction of the 60,000-seat stadium at Stanley Park. The design allows for the capacity to be increased to 73,000 if required. Original plans envisaged the ground being completed for the start of the 2011/12 season but it was announced in late 2008 that the club was delaying construction for at least 12 months as a result of the credit crunch and the loss of funds from the European Regional Development Fund that had originally been allocated for the regeneration of the Anfield area.

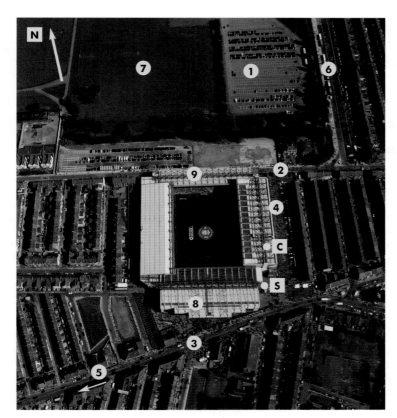

C Club Offices
S Club Shop

1 Car Park
2 Anfield Road
3 A5089 Walton Breck Road
4 Kemlyn Road
5 Kirkdale BR Station
  (1 mile)
6 Utting Avenue
7 Stanley Park
8 Spion Kop
9 Anfield Road Stand

⬆ *North direction (approx)*

◄ 702114
▼ 702108

macclesfield town

Moss Rose Ground, London Road, Macclesfield, SK11 7SP

website: **WWW.MTFC.CO.UK**
e:mail: **OFFICE@MTFC.CO.UK**
tel no: **01625 264686**
colours: **ROYAL BLUE SHIRTS, ROYAL BLUE SHORTS**
nickname: **THE SILKMEN**
season 2009/10: **LEAGUE TWO**

Last Season: **20th** (p**46**; w**13**; d**8**; l**25**; gf**45**; ga**77**)

One of a number of teams to be thankful, come the end of the season, that the pressure had been largely off in the relegation battle as a result of the fact that a number of teams – most notably given the relegation battle – Bournemouth and Luton had started the season in negative territory, the Silkmen would have faced a serious struggle to maintain their League status had neither Bournemouth nor Luton gone into Administration during 2008. As it was, Keith Alexander's team finished in 20th place, one point and one place worse than that achieved in 2007/08. It was not until the fifth League match of the season when the team secured their first points, ironically with a 2-1 victory at Moss Rose over Luton, but form thereafter was too inconsistent to achieve significant progress up the League Two table. Three wins and two draws in the club's final 14 League games of the season after an impressive 3-0 victory at home over promotion-chasing Shrewsbury Town saw the team drift down from 16th position. With all teams, at the time of writing, starting off on a level playing field, it's hard to escape a conclusion that Town may well again struggle to survive in the League come the end of the 2009/10 season.

Advance Tickets Tel No: 01625 264686
Fax: 01625 264692
Training Ground: Details omitted at club's request
Brief History: Founded 1874. Previous ground: Rostron Field moved to Moss Rose Ground in 1891. Winners of the Vauxhall Conference in 1994/95 and 1996/97. Admitted to Football League for 1997/98 season. Record attendance 10,041
(Total) Current Capacity: 6,335; (2,599 seated)
Visiting Supporters' Allocation: 1,900 (1,500 in Silkman Terrace; 400 seated in Estate Road Stand)
Nearest Railway Station: Macclesfield
Parking (Car): No parking at the ground and the nearest off-street car park is in the town centre (25min walk). There is some on-street parking in the vicinity, but this can get crowded.
Parking (Coach/Bus): As directed
Police Force and Tel No: Cheshire (01625 610000)
Disabled Visitors' Facilities:
Wheelchairs: 45 places in Estate Road Stand
Blind: No special facility
Anticipated Development(s): The club is examining the possibility of relocating to a new 10,000-capacity stadium as part of the Dane's Moss redevelopment.

C Club Offices
E Entrance(s) for visiting
   supporters

1 A523 London Road
2 To Town Centre and BR
   station (1.5 miles)
3 To Leek
4 Moss Lane
5 Star Lane
6 Site of Silkmans Public
   House (now demolished)
7 Star Lane End
8 Silkman End (away section)
9 Estate Road Stand

↑ North direction (approx)

◄ 700602
▼ 700598

manchester city

The City of Manchester Stadium, Sportcity, Manchester M11 3FF

website: **WWW.MCFC.CO.UK**
e:mail: **MCFC@MCFC.CO.UK**
tel no: **0870 062 1894**
colours: **SKY BLUE SHIRTS, WHITE SHORTS**
nickname: **THE BLUES**
season 2009/10: **PREMIER LEAGUE**

Last Season: **10th** (p**38**; w**15**; d**5**; l**18**; gf**58**; ga**50**)

Appointed only in the summer of 2008, Mark Hughes faced an almost immediate revolution at Manchester City when Thaksin Shinawatra sold the club to a Middle Eastern consortium based in Abu Dhabi. The club, historically regarded as the poor relation financially of Manchester United, now found itself portrayed as the wealthiest club in the world – an unfortunate accolade as buying prices tend to escalate if the seller perceives there to be virtually unlimited funds. The purchase came too late to have a dramatic impact on the club's pre-season activity, with the Brazilian star Robinho becoming the highest-profile arrival. On the field, City had a relatively mediocre season, inevitably heightening speculation about Hughes' future given the undoubted ambition of the club's new owners. Finishing mid-table, outside the Europa League positions, will undoubtedly be seen as a disappointment but on the field the club's performances were too variable ever to sustain a serious challenge for a top-seven place. Occasional strong results, such as the 3-0 victory at Eastlands over Arsenal and the 6-0 thrashing of Portsmouth, were countered by defeats away at struggling Middlesbrough, Stoke and West Bromwich. In the cup competitions, the team had some success in the UEFA Cup before losing to Hamburg in the Quarter-Finals but City was to suffer an embarrassing defeat away at League One Brighton, on penalties, in the Third Round of the Carling Cup. For 2009/10 it has been confirmed that Hughes will again be the manager; his position, and that of the club, will depend significantly on the success he has in bringing high-profile talent to the club and the team's start to the season. With the financial backing and expectations of the new owners to the fore, a top-sixth finish must be regarded as a prerequisite if the current regime is to survive.

Advance Tickets Tel No: 0870 062 1894

Fax: 0161 438 7999

Training Ground: Platt Lane Complex, Yew Tree Road, Fallowfield, Manchester M14 7UU;
Tel: 0161 248 6610; Fax: 0161 257 0030

Brief History: Founded 1880 at West Gorton, changed name to Ardwick (reformed 1887) and to Manchester City in 1894. Former grounds: Clowes Street (1880-81), Kirkmanshulme Cricket Club (1881-82), Queens Road (1882-84), Pink Bank Lane (1884-87), Hyde Road (1887-1923) and Maine Road (from 1923 until 2003). Moved to the City of Manchester Stadium for the start of the 2003/04 season. Founder-members 2nd Division (1892). Record attendance (at Maine Road) 84,569 (record for a Football League Ground); at City of Manchester Stadium 47,726

(Total) Current Capacity: 48,000

Visiting Supporters' Allocation: 3,000 (South Stand); can be increased to 4,500 if required

Nearest Railway Station: Manchester Piccadilly

Parking (Car): Ample match day parking available to the north of the stadium, entrance via Alan Turing Way. On-street parking restrictions operate in all areas adjacent to the stadium on matchdays.

Parking (Coach/Bus): Coach parking for visiting supporters is adjacent to turnstiles at Key 103 Stand. For home supporters to the north of the stadium, entrance from Alan Turing Way.

Police Force and Tel No: Greater Manchester (0161 872 5050)

Disabled Visitors' facilities:

Wheelchairs: 300 disabled seats around ground
Blind: 14 places alongside helpers in East Stand Level 1. Commentary available via headsets.

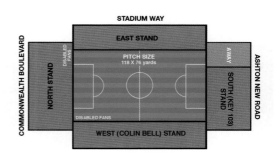

1. A662 Ashton New Road
2. Commonwealth Boulevard
3. Stadium Way
4. A6010 Alan Turing Way
5. North Stand
6. South (Key 103) Stand
7. West (Colin Bell) Stand
8. East Stand
9. National Squash Centre
10. Warm-up track
11. To Manchester city centre and Piccadilly station (1½ miles)

↑ North direction (approx)

◄ 701776
▼ 701787

107

manchester united

Old Trafford, Sir Matt Busby Way, Manchester, M16 0RA

website: **WWW.MANUTD.COM**
e:mail: **ENQUIRIES@MANUTD.CO.UK**
tel no: **0161 868 8000**
colours: **RED SHIRTS, WHITE SHORTS**
nickname: **THE RED DEVILS**
season 2009/10: **PREMIER LEAGUE**

Last Season: **1st** (p**38**; w**28**; d**6**; l**4**; gf**68**; ga**24**)

In many respects a disappointing conclusion to the season at Old Trafford – that is, if winning two domestic trophies (the Premier League and the Carling Cup) can be regarded as disasters – given that the team's domestic domination failed to translate itself into becoming the first team to retain the Champions League since the competition was reformed. If there was one defining match in the club's season it was undoubtedly the Champions League Final in Rome. Having comprehensively swept Arsenal aside in the Semi-Final, United faced Barcelona, the conquerors of Chelsea. Although United started the final brightly, the Spanish side scored first and thereafter controlled the match, eventually winning 2-0. It wasn't just the defeat that underscored the growing gap between the best in Britain and the best in Spain but the fact that the United management team didn't seem to be able to change the game plan in the face of Barcelona's skilful play. With players like Giggs and Scholes now in the twilight of their careers and with the departure of Ronaldo, there is an undoubted air of an end of an era in a team that has dominated English football since the inception of the Premier League. Undoubtedly in 2009/10 Sir Alex Ferguson's team will be the one to beat in all competitions but for a manager who wants to see his team equally dominant in Europe the challenge will be to strengthen the squad to build a team capable of competing with players like Iniesta, Messi, Xavi, Puyol and Henry who gave United a lesson in football in Rome.

Advance Tickets Tel No: 0161 868 8000

Fax: 0161 868 8804

Training Ground: Carrington Training Complex, Birch Road, Manchester M31 4HH

Brief History: Founded in 1878 as 'Newton Heath L&Y', later Newton Heath, changed to Manchester United in 1902. Former Grounds: North Road, Monsall & Bank Street, Clayton, moved to Old Trafford in 1910 (used Manchester City F.C. Ground 1941-49). Founder-members Second Division (1892). Record attendance 76,962

(Total) Current Capacity: 76,100 (all seated)

Visiting Supporters' Allocation: Approx. 3,000 in corner of South and East Stands

Nearest Railway Station: At Ground

Parking (Car): Lancashire Cricket Ground and White City

Parking (Coach/Bus): As directed by Police

Police Force and Tel No: Greater Manchester (0161 872 5050)

Disabled Visitors' Facilities:

Wheelchairs: South East Stand

Blind: Commentary available

Anticipated Development(s): The work on the £45 million project to construct infills at the north-east and north-west corners of the ground has now been completed and takes Old Trafford's capacity to 76,000, making it by some margin the largest league ground in Britain. Any future development of the ground will involve the Main (South) Stand although work here is complicated by the proximity of the building to the adjacent railway line.

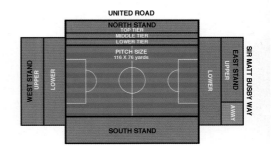

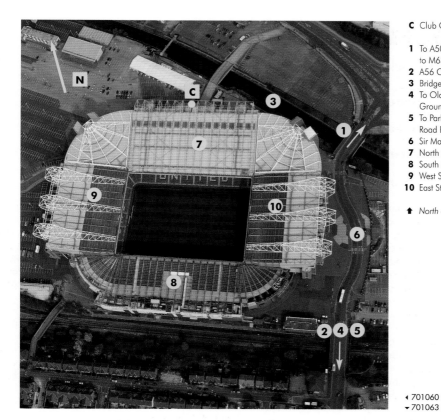

C Club Offices

1 To A5081 Trafford Park Road to M63 Junction 4 (5 miles)
2 A56 Chester Road
3 Bridgewater Canal
4 To Old Trafford Cricket Ground
5 To Parking and Warwick Road BR Station
6 Sir Matt Busby Way
7 North Stand
8 South Stand
9 West Stand
10 East Stand

↑ North direction (approx)

◄ 701060
▼ 701063

middlesbrough

Riverside Stadium, Middlesbrough, Cleveland TS3 6RS

website: **WWW.MFC.CO.UK**
e:mail: **ENQUIRIES@MFC.CO.UK**
tel no: **0844 499 6789**
colours: **RED SHIRTS, RED SHORTS**
nickname: **BORO**
season 2009/10: **CHAMPIONSHIP**

Last Season: **19th** (relegated) (p**38**; w**7**; d**11**; l**20**; gf**28**; ga**57**)

A fixture in the Premier League for 11 seasons, Boro's season ultimately turned into a disaster. Initially, the team under Gareth Southgate seemed to be heading for a position of mid-table stability but as the campaign wore on so the team's form – and in particular its ability to score goals – seemed to disappear and the club drifted down the Premier League table. A run of eight matches without a win up to the away defeat at Old Trafford saw the team just outside the drop zone at the end of the year and, despite an encouraging 2-0 home victory over Liverpool that seemed to suggest that the team might escape from the drop, the team's away form was lamentable and, although relegation wasn't finally confirmed until the last Sunday of the season, it would have required a significant away victory at West Ham allied with results elsewhere to have seen Boro' survive. As it was, Boro's defeat – one of 15 away from the Riverside Stadium – meant that results elsewhere were academic and consigned the team to spending 2009/10 in the Championship. The last time that Boro' made the drop, the team made an immediate return and the team will undoubtedly be one of the favourites for promotion. At the time of writing, Southgate has confirmed his intention to remain in charge for the new season; his challenge will be to acquire players to replace those who will undoubtedly leave as a result of relegation and, most importantly, acquire a proven goal scorer capable of converting the team's undoubtedly good play into victories.

Advance Tickets Tel No: 0844 499 1234
Fax: 01642 757690
Training Ground: Rockcliffe Park, Hurworth Place, Near Darlington, County Durham DL2 2DU; Tel: 01325 722222
Brief History: Founded 1876. Former Grounds: Archery Ground (Albert Park), Breckon Hill Road, Linthorpe Road, moved to Ayresome Park in 1903, and to current ground in Summer 1995. F.A. Amateur Cup winners 1894 and 1897 (joined Football League in 1899). Record attendance (Ayresome Park) 53,596, (Riverside Stadium) 35,000
(Total) Current Capacity: 35,100 (all seated)
Visiting Supporters' Allocation: 3,450 (in the South Stand)
Nearest Railway Station: Middlesbrough
Parking (Car): All parking at stadium is for permit holders
Parking (Coach/Bus): As directed
Police Force and Tel No: Cleveland (01642 248184)
Disabled Visitors' Facilities:
Wheelchairs: More than 170 places available for disabled fans
Blind: Commentary available
Anticipated Development(s): There remain long-term plans for the ground's capacity to be increased to 42,000 through the construction of extra tiers on the North, South and East stands, although there is no confirmed timetable for this work at the current time.

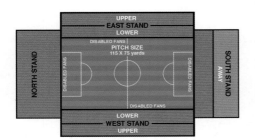

▲ 700627
◄ 700621

C Club Offices
S Club Shop

1 Cargo Fleet Road
2 To Middlesbrough
railway station
3 To Middlesbrough
town centre
4 Middlesbrough Docks
5 Shepherdson Way to A66
6 South Stand
7 Car parks

↑ *North direction (approx)*

millwall

The Den, Zampa Road, London, SE16 3LN

website: **WWW.MILLWALLFC.CO.UK**
e:mail: **QUESTIONS@MILLWALLPLC.COM**
tel no: **020 7232 1222**
colours: **BLUE SHIRTS, WHITE SHORTS**
nickname: **THE LIONS**
season 2009/10: **LEAGUE ONE**

STOCKHOLM ROAD

BOLINA ROAD

Last Season: **5th** (p**46**; w**25**; d**7**; l**14**; gf**63**; ga**53**)

Under Kenny Jackett, in his first full season in charge of the club, Millwall started relatively slowly but a run of 12 wins in 16 League matches took the team into the top two in mid-December and thereafter the Lions were in the hunt for automatic promotion right through until the end of the campaign. In the event, however, Leicester and Peterborough secured the two automatic places leaving Millwall to face the Play-Offs and a tricky Semi-Final against Leeds United. A 1-0 home victory gave the Londoners a slight edge for the return match at Elland Road and a hard-fought 1-1 draw in Yorkshire resulted in Millwall facing Scunthorpe United at Wembley in the Final. Falling behind to an early goal, Millwall established a 2-1 lead by half time only for the Iron to score two late goals to win the tie 3-2 and thus consign the Lions to another season in League One. With a number of ex-Premier League teams relegated to League One at the end of 2008/09, these teams will be undoubtedly fancied to make an immediate return to the Championship and the best that Jackett's team can perhaps look forward to is another push towards the Play-Offs.

Advance Tickets Tel No: 020 7231 9999
Fax: 020 7231 3663
Training Ground: Millwall FC Training Ground, Calmont Road (off Ashgrove Road), Bromley Hill, Bromley, Kent BR1 4BZ
Brief History: Founded 1885 as Millwall Rovers, changed name to Millwall Athletic (1889) and Millwall (1925). Former Grounds: Glengall Road, East Ferry Road (two separate Grounds), North Greenwich Ground and The Den – Cold Blow Lane – moved to New Den 1993/94 season. Founder-members Third Division (1920). Record attendance: (at The Den) 48,672; (at New Den) 20,093
(Total) Current Capacity: 20,150 (all seated)
Visiting Supporters' Allocation: 4,000 in North Stand
Nearest Railway Station: South Bermondsey or Surrey Docks (Tube)
Parking (Car): Juno Way car parking (8 mins walk)
Parking (Coach/Bus): At Ground
Police Force and Tel No: Metropolitan (0207 679 9217)
Disabled Visitors' Facilities:
Wheelchairs: 200 spaces in West Stand Lower Tier
Blind: Commentary available

C Club Offices
S Club Shop
E Entrance(s) for visiting
   supporters

1 Bolina Road
2 South Bermondsey station
3 Footpath to station for away
   fans
4 Zampa Road
5 Stockholm Road
6 North Stand (away)

↑ *North direction (approx)*

◄ 701493
▼ 701509

milton keynes dons

Stadium: MK, Denbigh, Milton Keynes, MK1 1SA

website: **WWW.MKDONS.COM**
e:mail: **INFO@MKDONS.COM**
tel no: **01908 622922**
colours: **WHITE SHIRTS, WHITE SHORTS**
nickname: **THE DONS**
season 2009/10: **LEAGUE ONE**

Last Season: **3rd** (p**46**; w**26**; d**9**; l**11**; gf**83**; ga**47**)

Promoted at the end of the 2007/08 season, MK Dons – like fellow arrival in League One Peterborough United – were determined to achieve two promotions in two seasons and, for much of the campaign, it looked as though Roberto di Matteo's team would seize one of the automatic promotion places. A strong start to the season – which included a 1-0 home victory over Championship side Norwich City in the First Round of the Carling Cup – saw the Dons in the Play-Off zone and for the bulk of the season the club was one of those vying to join Leicester City – the division's runaway leader – in promotion. However, from the middle of February, when the club stood second, some seven points clear of Peterborough in third, a run of four straight draws saw the chasing pack catch up. Ultimately, Posh finished second and the Dons third and thus faced Scunthorpe United in the Play-Offs. A 1-1 draw at Glanford Park seemed to give the Dons the edge but a 0-0 draw at home after extra time resulted in the match going to penalties, which the team from North Lincolnshire won 7-6. Thus the Dons face a second season in League One; the facilities and the team certainly have the potential and ambition to support football at a higher level and so should once again feature in the race for either automatic promotion or the Play-Offs. However, the club will face the challenge under a returned Paul Ince as di Matteo departed at the end of June to take over at West Brom.

Advance Tickets Tel No: 01908 622900
Fax: 01908 622933
Training Ground: Woughton on the Green, Milton Keynes
Brief History: Founded 1889 as Wimbledon Old Centrals, changed name to Wimbledon in 1905 and to Milton Keynes Dons in 2004. Former grounds: Wimbledon Common, Pepy's Road, Grand Drive, Merton Hall Road, Malden Wanderers Cricket Ground, Plough Lane, Selhurst Park (1991-2002) and National Hockey Stadium (2002-2007); moved to Stadium: MK for start of the 2007/08 season. Elected to the Football League in 1977. Record attendance (Plough Lane) 18,000; (Selhurst Park) 30,115; (National Hockey Stadium) 5,306; (Stadium: MK) 20,222
(Total) Current Capacity: 22,000 (all seated)
Visiting Supporters' Allocation: c3000 in northeast corner
Nearest Railway Station: Bletchley (two miles); Milton Keynes Central (four miles)
Parking (Car): The ground is located within a retail development and parking restrictions at the ground will probably apply.
Parking (Coach/Bus): As directed
Police Force and Tel No: Thames Valley Police (01865 846000)
Disabled Visitors' Facilities:
Wheelchairs: 164 spaces
Blind: No special facility
Anticipated Development(s): Following a number of years at the National Hockey Stadium, the Milton Keynes Dons moved into the new Stadium: MK for the start of the 2007/08 season. The ground has been designed to facilitate the addition of a second tier of seating if required in the future, taking the total capacity to 30,000.

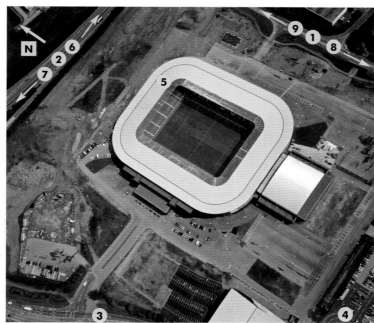

1 B4034 Saxon Street
2 A5
3 Grafton Street
4 Bletcham Way
5 Away Area
6 A5 Southbound to London
7 A5 Northbound to Milton
   Keynes centre and Towcester
8 To Bletchley railway station
   (two miles)
9 To Milton Keynes Central
   railway station (four miles)

⬆ North direction (approx)

◀ 702717
▼ 702730

morecambe

Christie Park, Lancaster Road, Morecambe, Lancashire, LA4 5TJ

website: **WWW.MORECAMBEFC.COM**
e:mail: **OFFICE@MORECAMBEFC.COM**
tel no: **01524 411797**
colours: **RED SHIRTS, WHITE SHORTS**
nickname: **SHRIMPS**
season 2009/10: **LEAGUE TWO**

Last Season: **11th (p46; w15; d18; l13; gf53; ga56)**

The Shrimps' third season in the Football League saw Sammy McIlroy's Morecambe secure another top-half finish – 11th as in 2007/08 – but it could have been much better as, for much of the campaign, it looked as though the team might have been a dark horse to sneak into the Play-Offs after a dire start to the season, which saw the club fail to win in its first five League games. A late run saw the team come within three points of the Play-Offs by mid-April but a further failure to win in the last three League matches saw the team drift away from seventh place. For 2009/10, Morecambe again has the potential for a top-half finish.

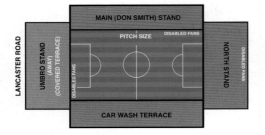

Advance Tickets Tel No: 01524 411797
Fax: 01524 832230
Training Ground: Address omitted at club's request
Brief History: Founded 1920. Previous grounds: Morecambe Cricket Ground; moved to Roseberry Park 1921; ground later renamed Christie Park after the club's president who had funded its purchase. Joined Conference at the end of the 1995/96 season and promoted to the Football League at the end of the 2006/07 season. Record attendance 9,234
(Total) Current Capacity: 6,400; (1,200 seated)
Visiting Supporters' Allocation: 1,500 (Umbro Stand – all standing) plus limited number of seats in Main Stand
Nearest Railway Station: Morecambe
Parking (Car): Main car park is pass only; there is a second small car park otherwise on-street only
Parking (Coach/Bus): As directed
Other clubs sharing ground: Blackburn Rovers Reserves
Police Force and Tel No: Lancashire Constabulary (0845 125 3545)
Disabled Visitors' Facilities:
Wheelchairs: 36 home and 10 away spaces
Blind: No special facility
Anticipated Development(s): Having previously announced plans to redevelop Christie Park, the club has now decided to relocate to a new 6,000-seater stadium. If all had gone according o plan, the new stadium could have been available for the start of the 2009/10 season but during the summer of 2008 the club announced a 12-month delay on the project with a new completion date of the start of the 2010/11 season. The construction of the new 6,800-seat ground at Westgate was given planning permission in September 2008. In order to fulfil League requirements, the club must provide 2,000 covered seats by the end of the 2009/10 season. In furtherance of the scheme, it was announced that Sainsbury's would purchase Christie Park and construct a new supermarket on the site. Work on the new ground was scheduled to start in April 2009.

1 B5321 Lancaster Road
2 Lathom Avenue
3 Christie Avenue
4 To Morecambe town centre and railway station (one mile)
5 To A589
6 Ennerdale Avenue
7 Roseberry Avenue
8 Burlington Avenue
9 North Stand
10 Main Stand
11 Umbro Stand (away)
12 Car Wash Terrace

↑ *North direction (approx)*

◄ 700865
▼ 700870

newcastle united

St James's Park, Newcastle-upon-Tyne, NE1 4ST

website: **WWW.NUFC.PREMIUMTV.CO.UK**
e:mail: **CONTACT VIA WEBSITE**
tel no: **0191 201 8400**
colours: **BLACK AND WHITE STRIPED SHIRTS, WHITE SHORTS**
nickname: **THE MAGPIES**
season 2009/10: **CHAMPIONSHIP**

Last Season: **18th** (relegated) (p**38**; w**7**; d**13**; l**18**; gf**40**; ga**59**)

With Newcastle United it's hard to know whether it's a tragedy or a farce as the season ultimately concluded with the club up for sale and relegated to the Championship. In early September, just after the closure of the transfer window, it was announced that Kevin Keegan had departed from St James's Park after only some eight months into the job. Coming back to the club for the second time following the dismissal of the unpopular Sam Allardyce, Keegan had initially struggled to get the team to perform but ultimately the Magpies had finished the 2007/08 season in mid-table; Keegan had, however, expressed his concerns over the club's direction and its ability to compete with the top spenders and, during the close season, United lost a number of players, including James Milner, and struggled to recruit. In last year's edition of this book we described the managerial role at Newcastle United as a poisoned chalice and little that has happened this year would suggest that the position has improved. Chris Hughton took over as caretaker, seeing the team lose 2-1 at home to promoted Hull City in his first game in charge. Towards the end of the month, with the crisis-hit club bumped out of the Carling Cup at St James's Park by Tottenham Hotspur and up for sale, the experienced Joe Kinnear was brought in as temporary boss. Kinnear's health meant that he was he was side-lined once it became obvious that he was going to undergo heart surgery and, with eight League matches left, one of the local heroes – Alan Shearer – was brought in to try and save United's Premier League status. However, a run of only one victory in the first seven games – a vital 3-1 victory over fellow strugglers Middlesbrough – meant relegation was likely unless the team could better the result of Hull City at home against Manchester United. Although Hull did their bit, losing 1-0, a tame 1-0 defeat at Villa Park saw United relegated after 16 seasons in the top tier. At the time of writing it's uncertain as to whether Shearer will still be in charge for the new season – he initially signed on only for the remainder of the 2008/09 season – but whoever is in charge will inherit a club that ought to be one of the top contenders for automatic promotion but, with the soap opera that is life at the club, anything is possible.

Advance Tickets Tel No: 0191 261 1571
Fax: 0191 201 8600
Training Ground: Darsley Park, Whitley Road, Benton, Newcastle upon Tyne NE12 9FA
Brief History: Founded in 1882 as Newcastle East End, changed to Newcastle United in 1892. Former Grounds: Chillingham Road, moved to St. James' Park (former home of defunct Newcastle West End) in 1892. Record attendance 68,386
(Total) Current Capacity: 52,387 (all seated)
Visiting Supporters' Allocation: 3,000 in North West Stand
Nearest Railway Station: Newcastle Central
Parking (Car): Leazes car park and street parking
Parking (Coach/Bus): Leazes car park
Police Force and Tel No: Northumbria (0191 232 3451)
Disabled Visitors' Facilities:
Wheelchairs: 103 spaces available
Blind: Commentary available
Anticipated Development(s): The club announced plans in March 2007 for a £300 million scheme to increase capacity at St James' Park to 60,000. The work, which would include the construction of a hotel and conference city, will see the expansion of the Gallow Gate End. The project, which has yet to receive planning consent, has no confirmed timescale at present.

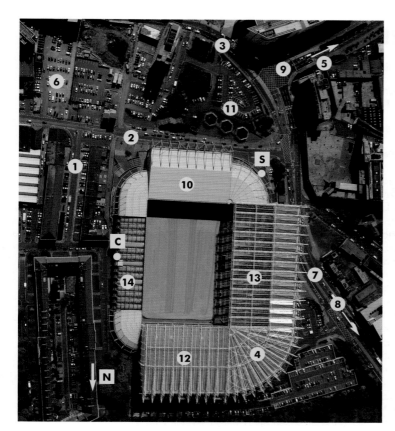

C Club Offices
S Club Shop

1 St. James's Park
2 Strawberry Place
3 Gallowgate
4 Away Section
5 To Newcastle Central BR
  Station ($1/2$ mile) &
  A6127(M)
6 Car Park
7 Barrack Road (A189)
8 To A1 and North
9 Corporation Street
10 Gallowgate End
11 Metro Station
12 Sir John Hall Stand
13 Millburn Stand
14 East Stand

↑ North direction (approx)

◄ 700356
▼ 700351

northampton town

Sixfields Stadium, Northampton, NN5 5QA

website: **WWW.NTFC.CO.UK**
e:mail: **PAULA.KANE@NTFC.TV**
tel no: **01604 683700**
colours: **CLARET WITH WHITE SLEEVED SHIRTS, WHITE SHORTS**
nickname: **THE COBBLERS**
season 2009/10: **LEAGUE TWO**

Last Season: **21st** (relegated) (p**46**; w**12**; d**13**; l**21**; gf**61**; ga**65**)

Ultimately, a disappointing season that sees the Cobblers drop back into English football's fourth tier after only three seasons in League One was the result of an appalling run of form that saw the team drop rapidly from mid-table at the end of January to 21st come the final set of results. The final 20 games of the season saw the team win only four games and draw four. Despite this run of form, the team might still have survived in League One had results gone their way on the final Saturday. One of effectively four teams that could have filled the final relegation spot – the others were Hartlepool, Brighton and Carlisle – if the Cobblers could have gained at least a point at Leeds United then Carlisle would have been relegated whatever their result against Millwall. Unfortunately, however, Stuart Gray's team lost 3-0 and thus dropped into the bottom four. As a relegated team, the Cobblers should have the potential to do well at the lower level and the Play-Offs should be a realistic expectation for the 2009/10 season.

Advance Tickets Tel No: 01604 683777
Fax: 01604 751613
Training Ground: No specific facility
Brief History: Founded 1897. Former, County, Ground was part of Northamptonshire County Cricket Ground. Moved to Sixfields Stadium during early 1994/95 season. Record attendance 24,523 (at County Ground); 7,557 (at Sixfields)
(Total) Current Capacity: 7,653 (all seated)
Visiting Supporters' Allocation: 850 (in Paul Cox Panel and Paint South Stand; can be increased to 1,150 if necessary)
Nearest Railway Station: Northampton
Parking (Car): Adjacent to Ground
Parking (Coach/Bus): Adjacent to Ground
Police Force and Tel No: Northants (01604 700700)
Disabled Visitors' Facilities:
Wheelchairs: Available on all four sides
Blind: Available
Anticipated Development(s): The club has plans to increase the capacity of the Sixfields Stadium to c16,000 all-seated although there is no timescale for this work.

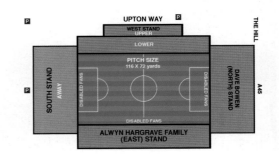

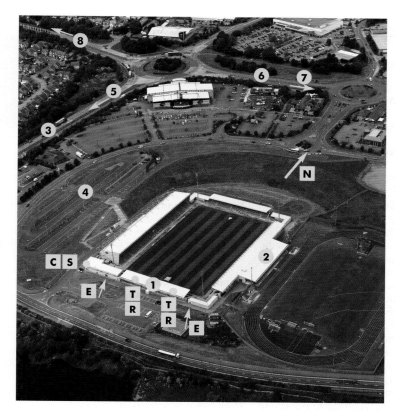

C Club Offices
S Club Shop
E Entrance(s) for visiting
   supporters
R Refreshment bars for visiting
   supporters
T Toilets for visiting supporters

1 South Stand (away)
2 Athletics Stand
3 Upton Way
4 Car parks
5 A45 towards A43
  (Towcester and A5)
6 Weedon Road
7 To Town Centre and station
8 A45 to M1 (Jct 16)

↑ North direction (approx)

◄ 702744
▼ 702750

norwich city

Carrow Road, Norwich, NR1 1JE

website: **WWW.CANARIES.CO.UK**
e:mail: **RECEPTION@NCFC-CANARIES.CO.UK**
tel no: **01603 760760**
colours: **YELLOW SHIRTS, GREEN SHORTS**
nickname: **THE CANARIES**
season 2009/10: **LEAGUE ONE**

Last Season: **22nd** (relegated) (p**46**; w**12**; d**10**; l**24**; gf**57**; ga**70**)

One of a number of ex-Premier League teams to find the 2008/09 season a struggle, Norwich City ultimately joined Southampton and Charlton Athletic in the drop to League One, heading back to the third tier of English football for the first time since promotion at the end of the 1959/60 season. Appointed during the 2007/08 season, Glenn Roeder was to guide the Canaries away from relegation during his first season in charge but found the new season to be more of a struggle although there were the occasional high points – such as the 5-2 victory at Carrow Road over promotion-chasing Wolverhampton Wanderers and a home win over local rivals Ipswich Town. During December, with assistant manager Lee Clark having departed to take over at Huddersfield, the Canaries gained only three out of a possible 12 points, dropping them towards the relegation zone, and the situation deteriorated further in January. Roeder was sacked and popular ex-keeper Bryan Gunn was brought in to replace him. Unfortunately, Gunn was unable to prevent the continuing slide and, ultimately, the club's fate depended on results on the final Saturday. Having lost 2-0 at home to Reading in their penultimate game, the Canaries needed to win at already-relegated Charlton and hope that Barnsley lost away to Plymouth. In the event, the 4-2 defeat at The Valley made the result at Home Park irrelevant and ensured that City will be playing in League One in 2009/10. Again, as one of the relegated teams, City should have the potential to make the Play-Offs at least but as other ex-Premier Leagues in this division – such as Leeds and Forest – have discovered it is by no means a certainty.

Advance Tickets Tel No: 0844 826 1902
Fax: 01603 613886
Training Ground: Colney Training Centre, Hethersett Lane, Colney, Norwich NR4 7TS
Brief History: Founded 1902. Former grounds: Newmarket Road and the Nest, Rosary Road; moved to Carrow Road in 1935. Founder-members 3rd Division (1920). Record attendance 43,984
(Total) Current Capacity: 26,034
Visiting Supporters' Allocation: 2,500 maximum in South Stand
Nearest Railway Station: Norwich
Parking (Car): City centre car parks
Parking (Coach/Bus): Lower Clarence Road
Police Force and Tel No: Norfolk (01603 768769)
Disabled Visitors' Facilities:
Wheelchairs: New facility in corner infill stand
Blind: Commentary available
Anticipated Development(s): The £3 million corner infill between the new Jarrold (South) Stand and the River End was opened in two stages in early 2005. The upper tier provides seats for 850 and the lower for 660. There is also a new disabled area located between the two tiers. This work takes Carrow Road's capacity to 26,000. As part of the plans for the Jarrold Stand, the pitch was relocated one metre away from the City Stand; this will facilitate the construction of a second tier on the City Stand in the future if required.

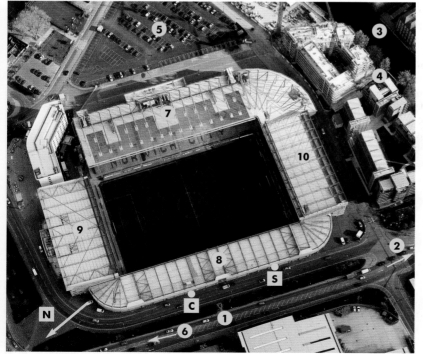

▲ 700801
◀ 700795

C Club Offices
S Club Shop

1 Carrow Road
2 A47 King Street
3 River Wensum
4 Riverside
5 Car Park
6 To Norwich BR Station
7 South (Jarrold) Stand
8 Geoffrey Watling (City) Stand
9 Barclay End Stand
10 The Norwich & Peterborough
(River End) Stand

↑ *North direction (approx)*

nottingham forest

City Ground, Nottingham, NG2 5FJ

website: **WWW.NOTTINGHAMFOREST.CO.UK**
e:mail: **ENQUIRIES@NOTTINGHAMFOREST.CO.UK**
tel no: **0115 982 4444**
colours: **RED SHIRTS, WHITE SHORTS**
nickname: **THE REDS**
season 2009/10: **CHAMPIONSHIP**

Last Season: **19th** (p**46**; w**13**; d**14**; l**19**; gf**50**; ga**65**)

Finishing second at the end of the 2007/08 season resulted in Championship football being restored to the City Ground for 2008/09. However, as with Doncaster Rovers, the enhanced status was to prove a considerable challenge for Forest and it was not until the end of the campaign that Championship status for 2009/10 was assured. On 26 December – following an embarrassing 4-2 home defeat to fellow strugglers Doncaster Rovers – the increasingly unpopular Colin Calderwood was sacked as manager; he was replaced immediately by the ex-Derby County boss Billy Davies. The new manager had an immediate effect, inspiring the team to an impressive 3-0 victory at Eastlands over Premier League Manchester City in the FA Cup and, under Davies, sufficient League points were gathered to ensure survival in the Championship. Davies has proved himself an astute operator at this level before and, with judicious strengthening of the squad, the club ought to be able to consolidate itself in the Championship. With strong teams emerging from League One, the scramble to avoid the drop from the Championship in 2009/10 is likely to go to the wire but Forest should have the nous to avoid relegation.

Advance Tickets Tel No: 0871 226 1980
Fax: 0115 982 4455
Training Ground: Nottingham Forest Football Academy, Gresham Close, West Bridgford, Nottingham NG2 7RQ
Brief History: Founded 1865 as Forest Football Club, changed name to Nottingham Forest (c1879). Former Grounds: Forest Recreation Ground, Meadow Cricket Ground, Trent Bridge (Cricket Ground), Parkside, Gregory Ground and Town Ground, moved to City Ground in 1898. Founder-members of Second Division (1892). Record attendance 49,945
(Total) Current Capacity: 30,602 (all seated)
Visiting Supporters' Allocation: Approx 4,750
Nearest Railway Station: Nottingham
Parking (Car): East car park and street parking
Parking (Coach/Bus): East car park
Police Force and Tel No: Nottinghamshire (0115 948 1888)
Disabled Visitors' Facilities:
Wheelchairs: Front of Brian Clough Stand
Blind: No special facility
Anticipated Development(s): In late June 2007 it was announced that the club was planning a possible relocation from the City Ground to a new 50,000-seat ground at Clifton. If all goes according to plan, the club anticipates moving into the new £45-50 million ground for the start of the 2014/15 season.

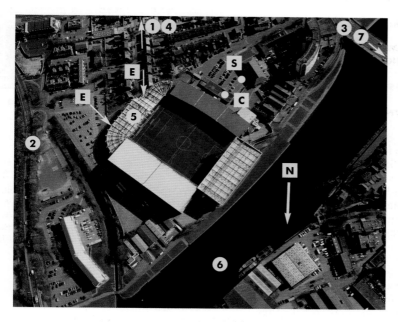

C Club Offices
S Club Shop
E Entrance(s) for visiting supporters

1 To Radcliffe Road
2 Lady Bay Bridge Road
3 Trent Bridge
4 To Trent Bridge Cricket Ground
5 Bridgford Stand
6 River Trent
7 To Nottingham Midland BR Station (½ mile)

↟ *North direction (approx)*

◄ 700807
▾ 700817

notts county

Meadow Lane, Nottingham, NG2 3HJ

website: **WWW.NOTTSCOUNTYFC.CO.UK**
e:mail: **INFO@NOTTSCOUNTYFC.CO.UK**
tel no: **0115 952 9000**
colours: **BLACK AND WHITE STRIPED SHIRTS, WHITE SHORTS**
nickname: **THE MAGPIES**
season 2009/10: **LEAGUE TWO**

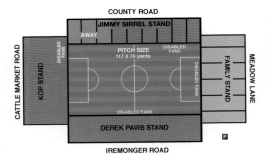

Last Season: **19th** (p**46**; w**11**; d**14**; l**21**; gf**49**; ga**69**)

In his first full season as boss of the Magpies, Ian McParland, a manager who'd had a long playing career with County in the 1980s when he scored 90 goals for the team in 267 appearances, guided the team to 19th place, a slight improvement on that achieved in 2007/08. At one point it looked as though a position of mid-table mediocrity beckoned as the club reached the dizzy heights of 15th at the end of February but a poor run towards the end of the campaign saw McParland's team achieve only two wins and two draws in the club's final 13 League matches. Given that two of the teams below County were Bournemouth and Luton – both of which had suffered a significant points deduction – County's 19th position was a shade false and, in 2009/10, the club may again be more interested in events at the bottom, rather than the top, of the division, although the arrival of new owners has brought an influx of new talent and renewed optimism to the club and its fans. And then there was Sven.

Advance Tickets Tel No: 0115 955 7204
Fax: 0115 955 3994
Training Ground: New facility being sought for 2009/10 season
Brief History: Founded 1862 (oldest club in Football League) as Nottingham, changed to Notts County in c1882. Former Grounds: Notts Cricket Ground (Beeston), Castle Cricket Ground, Trent Bridge Cricket Ground, moved to Meadow Lane in 1910. Founder-members Football League (1888). Record attendance 47,310
(Total) Current Capacity: 20,300 (all seated)
Visiting Supporters' Allocation: 1,300 in Jimmy Sirrel Stand
Nearest Railway Station: Nottingham Midland
Parking (Car): Mainly street parking
Parking (Coach/Bus): Cattle market
Police Force and Tel No: Nottingham (0115 948 1888)
Disabled Visitors' Facilities:
Wheelchairs: Meadow Lane/Jimmy Sirrel/Derek Pavis Stands
Blind: No special facility

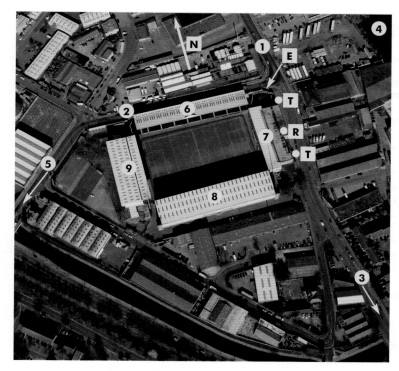

E Entrance(s) for visiting supporters
R Refreshment bars for visiting supporters
T Toilets for visiting supporters

1 A6011 Meadow Lane
2 County Road
3 A60 London Road
4 River Trent
5 Nottingham Midland BR Station ($^1/_2$ mile)
6 Jimmy Sirrel Stand
7 Family (Meadow Lane) Stand
8 Derek Pavis Stand
9 Kop Stand

↑ *North direction (approx)*

◄ 700818
▼ 700828

oldham athletic

Boundary Park, Oldham, OL1 2PA

website: **WWW.OLDHAMATHLETIC.CO.UK**
e:mail: **ENQUIRIES@OLDHAMATHLETIC.CO.UK**
tel no: **0871 226 2235**
colours: **BLUE SHIRTS, BLUE SHORTS**
nickname: **THE LATICS**
season 2009/10: **LEAGUE ONE**

Last Season: **10th** (p**46**; w**17**; d**16**; l**13**; gf**66**; ga**65**)

A good start to the season, with six wins and three draws from the first 10 League matches saw John Sheridan's team in the Play-Off places and vying for automatic promotion. However, in mid-March, following a 6-2 defeat by MK Dons and allegations of a brawl at the Belle Vue greyhound track, Sheridan departed with the team having slipped to eighth place in the table. Sheridan was replaced immediately by former boss Joe Royle who took over until the end of the season; under Royle, the team was unable to turn the club's fortunes around, with the team winning only one of the last nine League games of the season after the reverse at MK Dons. At the end of the season it was announced that Derek Penney, the ex-Darlington manager, was to take over for 2009/10. Penney is highly experienced at this level having had success with unfashionable teams such as Doncaster Rovers and he should have the ability to ensure again that the Latics are a force in League One.

Advance Tickets Tel No: 0871 226 1653
Fax: 0871 226 1715
Training Ground: Chapel Road, Hollins, Oldham OL8 4QQ
Brief History: Founded 1897 as Pine Villa, changed name to Oldham Athletic in 1899. Former Grounds: Berry's Field, Pine Mill, Athletic Ground (later named Boundary Park), Hudson Fold, moved to Boundary Park in 1906. Record attendance 47,671
(Total) Current Capacity: 10,900 (all seated)
Visiting Supporters' Allocation: 1,800 minimum, 4,600 maximum
Nearest Railway Station: Oldham Werneth
Parking (Car): Lookers Stand car park
Parking (Coach/Bus): At Ground
Other Clubs Sharing Ground: Oldham Roughyeads RLFC
Police Force and Tel No: Greater Manchester (0161 624 0444)
Disabled Visitors' Facilities:
Wheelchairs: Rochdale Road and Seton Stands
Blind: No special facility
Anticipated Development(s): The 1971-built Broadway Stand was demolished during the summer of 2008 with a new 5,200-seat stand due to replace it. Work on the replacement stand was scheduled to start during the first half of 2009 and results in a reduced capacity for the start of the new season. The redevelopment of the ground, aimed at creating a ground with a 16,000 capacity, will also include a hotel, fitness club and offices,

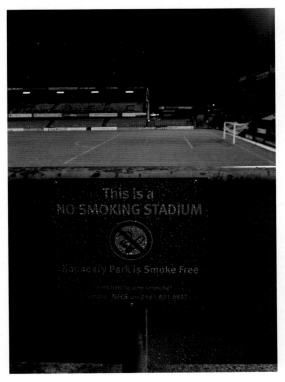

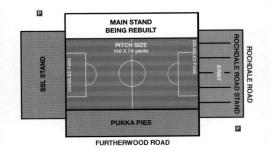

◄ 701803
▼ 701821

129

peterborough united

London Road, Peterborough, Cambs, PE2 8AL

website: **WWW.THEPOSH.COM**
e:mail: **INFO@THEPOSH.COM**
tel no: **01733 563947**
colours: **BLUE SHIRTS, WHITE SHORTS**
nickname: **POSH**
season 2009/10: **CHAMPIONSHIP**

Last Season: **2nd** (Promoted) (p**46**; w**26**; d**11**; l**9**; gf**78**; ga**54**)

Posh, although only promoted at the end of the 2007/08 season from League Two, were always destined to be in the mix for either automatic promotion or the Play-Offs come the end of the 2008/09 season. Ambitious both on the field and behind the scenes, Darren Ferguson's team had, however, a disappointing start to the season, winning only twice in their first eight League matches to leave the team in mid-table. By December, Posh had reached the Play-Off places and this form was to continue through to end of the season with promotion being guaranteed following the 1-0 home victory over Colchester United in the penultimate game of the season. Other clubs that have made a rapid ascent up the League have struggled often after a second successive promotion to sustain the status recently acquired; undoubtedly Posh will take some time to reacquaint themselves with the second tier of English football where the team hasn't played since relegation at the end of the 1993/94 season but the ambition of the club is such that the team ought to be able to ensure a reasonable mid-table finish.

Advance Tickets Tel No: 01733 865674
Fax: 01733 344140
Training Ground: Woodlands, Slash Lane, Castor, Peterborough PE5 7BD
Brief History: Founded in 1934 (no connection with former 'Peterborough and Fletton United' FC). Elected to Football League in 1960. Record attendance 30,096
(Total) Current Capacity: 15,314 (7,669 seated)
Visiting Supporters' Allocation: 4,758 (756 seated)
Nearest Railway Station: Peterborough
Parking (Car): Peterborough
Parking (Coach/Bus): At ground
Police Force and Tel No: Cambridgeshire (01733 563232)
Disabled Visitors' Facilities:
Wheelchairs: South Stand
Blind: No special facility
Future Development(s): The club announced in mid-January 2007 that it was examining the possibility of seeking planning permission to replace the existing terraced Moys End Stand with a new 2,000-seat stand as part of a five-year plan that could ultimately see London Road converted into an all-seater stadium.

GLEBE ROAD

NORWICH & PETERBOROUGH STAND
UPPER
DISABLED (D-WING)   LOWER
PITCH SIZE
112 X 71 yards

MOYS TERRACE (COVERED) AWAY

LONDON ROAD TERRACE (COVERED)

LONDON ROAD

ENCLOSURE   DISABLED

A STAND AWAY   MAIN STAND   WEST WING

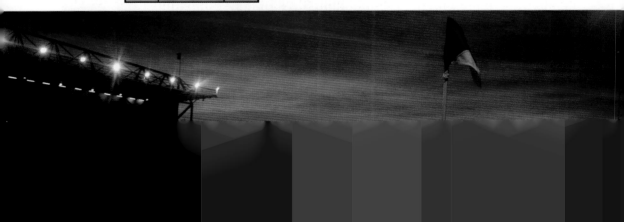

C Club Offices
S Club Shop
E Entrance(s) for visiting
supporters
R Refreshment bars for visiting
supporters
T Toilets for visiting supporters

1 A15 London Road
2 Car Parks
3 Peterborough BR Station
   (1 mile)
4 Glebe Road
5 A605
6 To A1 (north) (5 miles)
7 Main Stand
8 To Whittlesey
9 To A1 (south) (5 miles)
10 Norwich & Peterborough
   Stand
11 London Road Terrace
12 Moys Terrace (away)

↑ *North direction (approx)*

◀ 700652
▼ 700662

plymouth argyle

Home Park, Plymouth, PL2 3DQ

website: **WWW.PAFC.CO.UK**
e:mail: **ARGYLE@PAFC.CO.UK**
tel no: **01752 562561**
colours: **WHITE AND GREEN SHIRTS, GREEN SHORTS**
nickname: **THE PILGRIMS**
season 2009/10: **CHAMPIONSHIP**

Last Season: **21st** (p**46**; w**13**; d**12**; l**21**; gf**44**; ga**57**)

A dire start to the 2008/09 season, which saw the Pilgrims fail to win any of their first five League matches – leaving the club rock bottom of the Championship – in early September seemed to set the tempo for the season. However, a sudden reversal of form saw Paul Sturrock's team acquire 13 of the next 15 points and rise rapidly to the Play-Off places and as late as Boxing Day the club was still in mid-table. However, a further run of nine League games without a victory sent the team plunging down the table and an ongoing battle to avoid the drop. Ultimately, however, the club was to survive without any last day drama as Norwich's defeat at home to Reading on 26 April ensured that the Pilgrims had a five-point barrier between them and the East Anglian team. Without that defeat, the visit of equally threatened Barnsley to Home Park for the final game of the season would have been even more edgy. As it was the Tykes won 2-1 resulting in Argyle finishing 21st. For 2009/10 Sturrock's team probably faces another season of struggle and relegation is a real risk.

Advance Tickets Tel No: 0845 338 7232
Fax: 01752 606167
Training Ground: Adjacent to ground
Brief History: Founded 1886 as Argyle Athletic Club, changed name to Plymouth Argyle in 1903. Founder-members Third Division (1920). Record attendance 43,596
(Total) Current Capacity: 19,500 (all seated)
Visiting Supporters' Allocation: 1,300 (all seated) in Barn Park End Stand up to maximum of 2,000
Nearest Railway Station: Plymouth
Parking (Car): Car park adjacent
Parking (Coach/Bus): Central car park
Police Force and Tel No: Devon & Cornwall (0990 777444)
Disabled Visitors' Facilities:
Wheelchairs: Devonport End
Blind: Commentary available

Anticipated Development(s): Work on the three new stands at Home Park progressed well, with work being completed during the 2001/02 season. Plans, however, for the demolition of the existing Main Stand and its replacement have been resurrected as part of a £37 million redevelopment to create a three-tiered structure taking the ground to 18,600 (all-seated). There is no confirmed timescale for this work.

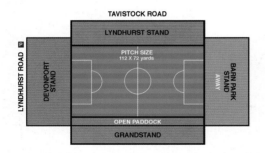

C Club Offices
S Club Shop

1 A386 Outland Road
2 Car Park
3 Devonport Road
4 Central Park
5 Town Centre & Plymouth BR
   Station (½ mile)
6 To A38 (½ mile)

⬆ *North direction (approx)*

◀ 701231
▾ 701234

portsmouth

Fratton Park, Frogmore Road, Southsea, Portsmouth, PO4 8RA

website: **WWW.PORTSMOUTHFC.CO.UK**
e:mail: **INFO@POMPEYFC.CO.UK**
tel no: **02392 731204**
colours: **BLUE SHIRTS, WHITE SHORTS**
nickname: **POMPEY**
season 2009/10: **PREMIER LEAGUE**

Last Season: **14th** (p**38**; w**10**; d**11**; l**17**; gf**38**; ga**57**)

Following the euphoria of the FA Cup victory in May 2008 and the promise of European football in 2008/09, hopes were high at Fratton Park that the new season would see further progress on the field. The reality, however, was very different. Towards the end of October, with Pompey secure in seventh place in the Premier League table, it was announced that Harry Redknapp, who had guided the team to its FA Cup triumph, was to depart to take over at struggling Tottenham Hotspur. The club acted quickly in appointing Tony Adams, Redknapp's assistant, as the club's new boss. However, the appointment was not to prove a success as results – two League wins out of 16 – resulted in the club's inexorable descent down the Premier League table. Adams, whose position wasn't aided by the sale of Lassana Diarra and Jermain Defoe in the January transfer window, was sacked in early February following the 3-2 home defeat by Liverpool that left Pompey in 16th position, one point above the drop zone. Paul Hart was appointed the new boss and under his guidance the club's position was stabilised and Premier League survival assured before the end of the campaign. The challenge for Hart will be to ensure that the club builds upon the stability that he brought. The squad, however, should be capable of ensuring a mid-table position in 2009/10.

Advance Tickets Tel No: 0844 847 1898
Fax: 02392 734129
Club Office: Rodney Road, Portsmouth, PO4 8SX
Training Ground: Stoneham Lane, Eastleigh SO50 9HT
Brief History: Founded 1898. Founder-members Third Division (1920). Record attendance 51,385
(Total) Current Capacity: 20,700 (all seated)
Visiting Supporters' Allocation: 2,000 (max) in Milton Stand
Nearest Railway Station: Fratton
Parking (Car): Street parking
Parking (Coach/Bus): As directed by Police
Police Force and Tel No: Hampshire (02392 321111)
Disabled Visitors' Facilities:
Wheelchairs: Fratton End
Blind: No special facility

Anticipated Development(s): The club's original plans for relocation to a site close to the city's naval dockyard brought objections from the Royal Navy and, as a result, the club identified a new site for the construction of a 36,000-seat ground at Horsea Island. Planning permission for the new ground was to be sought in 2008 with an original anticipated completion date of the start of the 2011/12 season. As a temporary measure a roof was installed over the Milton End during the 2007/08 season. However, the credit crunch has caused a rethink and, in early 2009, it was announced that in the short term the club would redevelop Fratton Park into a 30,000-seat ground. This work will entail rotating the pitch 90 degrees, the construction of two new stands, the enlargement of the Fratton End and improvement of the existing South Stand. If planning permission is gained, then work will start quickly to get the capacity up to 25,000 by the start of the 2010/11 season and to 30,000 by the start of the following season. The relocation scheme will, however, continue to be developed with a view to completion in 2018 and possible use should England gain the World Cup that year.

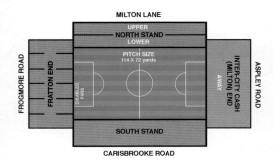

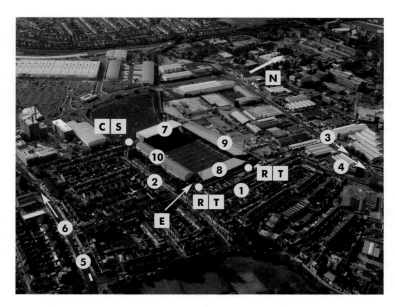

C Club Offices
S Club Shop
E Entrance(s) for visiting
   supporters
R Refreshment bars for visiting
   supporters
T Toilets for visiting supporters

1 Alverstone Road
2 Carisbrook Road
3 A288 Milton Road
4 To A27
5 Goldsmith Avenue
6 Fratton BR station
   (½ mile)
7 Fratton End
8 Milton End
9 North Stand
10 South Stand

⬆ *North direction (approx)*

◄ 701219
▼ 701226

port vale

Vale Park, Burslem, Stoke-on-Trent, ST6 1AW

website: **WWW.PORT-VALE.CO.UK**
e:mail: **ENQUIRIES@PORT-VALE.CO.UK**
tel no: **01782 655800**
colours: **WHITE SHIRTS, BLACK SHORTS**
nickname: **THE VALIANTS**
season 2009/10: **LEAGUE TWO**

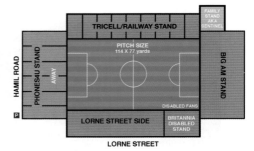

Appointed in November 2007 but unable to prevent the club's relegation to League Two, Lee Sinnott lasted less than a year as manager of Port Vale before being sacked in late September 2008 following a run of three defeats in four home games culminating in a 4-1 reverse against Macclesfield Town. Dean Glover took over as caretaker boss and was confirmed as the new permanent boss in early October. In his first League game, he took Vale to Shrewsbury – a club that had had an impressive home run until that point winning all their games at the ProStar Stadium and not conceding a goal – and came away with an impressive 2-1 victory despite finishing the game with only 10 players. However, Glover's reign was to be short-lived and, before the final match of the season, it was confirmed that his services would not be required for 2009/10. A combination of poor results – the team only won 11 of the 38 games under his control – and increasing disillusionment from the fans, reflected in poor season ticket sales, resulted in his departure. With the club looking to bring in new investment for the new season, and with the experienced Micky Adams now in charge, the Valiants ought to be one of the teams vying for a Play-Off place at least.

Advance Tickets Tel No: 01782 655832
Fax: 01782 834981
Training Ground: Adjacent to ground
Brief History: Founded 1876 as Burslem Port Vale, changed name to 'Port Vale' in 1907 (reformed club). Former Grounds: The Meadows Longport, Moorland Road Athletic Ground, Cobridge Athletic Grounds, Recreation Ground Hanley, moved to Vale Park in 1950. Founder-members Second Division (1892). Record attendance 49,768
(Total) Current Capacity: 18,471 (all seated)
Visiting Supporters' Allocation: 4,550
(in Hamil Road [Phones4U] Stand)
Nearest Railway Station: Longport (two miles)
Parking (Car): Car park at Ground
Parking (Coach/Bus): Hamil Road car park
Police Force and Tel No: Staffordshire (01782 577114)
Disabled Visitors' Facilities:
Wheelchairs: 20 spaces in new Britannic Disabled Stand
Blind: Commentary availaable
Anticipated Development(s): After some years of standing half completed, the club's new owners completed the roof over the Lorne Street Stand during the 2004/05 season. The Club had planned to install seats in the remainder of the stand during the 2007/08 season but this is still to be undertaken.

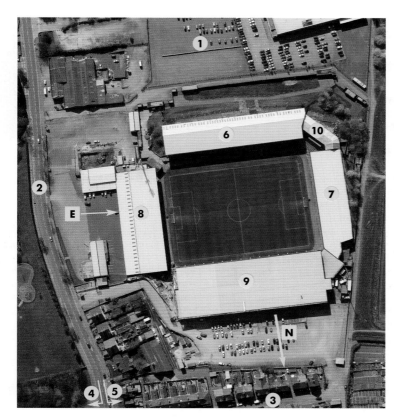

preston north end

Deepdale, Sir Tom Finney Way, Preston, PR1 6RU

website: **WWW.PNEFC.NET**
e:mail: **ENQUIRIES@PNE.COM**
tel no: **0844 856 1964**
colours: **WHITE SHIRTS, BLUE SHORTS**
nickname: **THE LILYWHITES**
season 2009/10: **CHAMPIONSHIP**

Last Season: **6th** (p**46**; w**21**; d**11**; l**14**; gf**66**; ga**54**)

Mid-table at the end of the 2007/08 season, under Alan Irvine North End had a much improved season in 2008/09 although it was not until the very end of the campaign that the team sneaked into the final Play-Off place. Following a 1-0 defeat by local rivals Blackpool, which left Irvine's team in eighth place some seven points off the all-important sixth spot with only four games left, it looked all but over but an impressive run of four victories in these matches culminating in a 2-1 victory over QPR at Deepdale in the last match of the season was enough to pip Cardiff City – defeated 1-0 at Sheffield Wednesday – to sixth on goal difference. However, a 1-1 draw with Sheffield United at home gave the South Yorkshire team the edge which was cemented when the Blades won 1-0 at Bramall Lane. Consigned, therefore, again to Championship football, the progress made in 2008/09 would suggest that again Preston might be a reasonable bet for the Play-Offs.

Advance Tickets Tel No: 0844 856 1966
Fax: 01772 693366
Training Ground: Springfields Sports Ground, Dodney Drive, Lea, Preston PR2 1XR
Brief History: Founded 1867 as a Rugby Club, changed to soccer in 1881. Former ground: Moor Park, moved to (later named) Deepdale in 1875. Founder-members Football League (1888). Record attendance 42,684
(Total) Current Capacity: 24,525 (all seated)
Visiting Supporters' Allocation: 6,000 maximum in Bill Shankly Stand
Nearest Railway Station: Preston (2 miles)
Parking (Car): West Stand car park
Parking (Coach/Bus): West Stand car park
Police Force and Tel No: Lancashire (01772 203203)
Disabled Visitors' Facilities:
Wheelchairs: Tom Finney Stand and Bill Shankly Stand
Blind: Earphones Commentary
Anticipated Development(s): Work started on the redevelopment of the fourth side of the ground in 2007. The new structure, destined to replace the Pavilion Stand of the 1930s, is named the Invincibles Pavilion in honour of the double-winning side of 1888/1889. The stand, which cost some £6 million, provides seating for 4,500 along with executive boxes, taking the ground's capacity to 24,000.

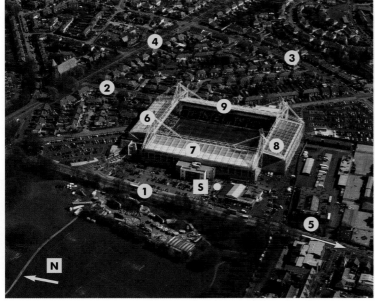

S Club Shop

1 A6033 Deepdale Road
2 Lowthorpe Road
3 Car Park
4 A5085 Blackpool Road
5 Preston BR Station
(2 miles)
6 Bill Shankly Stand
7 Tom Finney Stand
8 Town End Stand
9 Invincibles Pavilion stand

↑ *North direction (approx)*

queens park rangers

Loftus Road Stadium, South Africa Road, London, W12 7PA

website: **WWW.QPR.CO.UK**
e:mail: **BOXOFFICE@QPR.CO.UK**
tel no: **020 8743 0262**
colours: **BLUE AND WHITE HOOPED SHIRTS, WHITE SHORTS**
nickname: **THE SUPERHOOPS**
season 2009/10: **CHAMPIONSHIP**

Last Season: **11th** (p**46**; w**15**; d**16**; l**15**; gf**42**; ga**44**)

Taken over during 2008 by a consortium led by the Formula One boss Bernie Ecclestone, QPR appointed Iain Dowie before the start of the season and, with the big money backing, great things were expected from the team. The reality, however, was very different. Dowie survived in the job a handful of months before disagreements with co-owner Flavio Briatore led to his departure at the end of October with the team in ninth place, one point outside the Play-Off places. The club moved quickly to appoint Paulo Sousa, the Portuguese former midfielder, as new boss. Sousa's reign was not to be long as he was dismissed in early April after only 26 games in charge after he was accused of divulging confidential information. Under Sousa the club had slipped to 10th place. Player-coach Gareth Ainsworth was appointed caretaker boss until the end of the season. Outside of the League, QPR was to suffer an embarrassing defeat 2-1 away at League One Swindon Town. New manager Jim Magilton will have to face the heightened expectations that the new investment has brought but the Championship remains a competitive League given the imbalance resulting from the six clubs operating with the Premier League parachute payments and QPR will perhaps struggle to achieve more than a Play-Off place at best.

Advance Tickets Tel No: 0844 477 7007
Fax: 020 8749 0994
Training Ground: Imperial College Sports Ground, Sipson Lane, Harlington, Middlesex UB3 5AQ
Brief History: Founded 1885 as 'St. Jude's Institute', amalgamated with Christchurch Rangers to become Queens Park Rangers in 1886. Football League record number of former Grounds and Ground moves (13 different venues, 17 changes), including White City Stadium (twice) final move to Loftus Road in 1963. Founder-members Third Division (1920). Record attendance (at Loftus Road) 35,353
(Total) Current Capacity: 19,130 (all seated)
Visiting Supporters' Allocation: 2,500 (maximum)
Nearest Railway Station: Shepherds Bush and White City (both tube)
Parking (Car): White City NCP and street parking
Parking (Coach/Bus): White City NCP
Police Force and Tel No: Metropolitan (020 8741 6212)
Disabled Visitors' Facilities:
Wheelchairs: Ellerslie Road Stand and West Paddock
Blind: Ellerslie Road Stand
Anticipated Development(s): There is vague talk of possible relocation, but nothing has been confirmed. Given the constrained site occupied by Loftus Road, it will be difficult to increase the existing ground's capacity.

140

C Club Offices
S Club Shop
E Entrance(s) for visiting
  supporters

1 South Africa Road
2 To White City Tube Station,
  A219 Wood Lane and A40
  Western Avenue
3 A4020 Uxbridge Road
4 To Shepherds Bush Tube
  Station
5 To Acton Central Station
6 BBC Television Centre
7 Loftus Road
8 Bloemfontein Road

⬆ North direction (approx)

◄ 700895
▼ 700889

reading

Madejski Stadium, Bennet Road, Reading, RG2 0FL

website: **WWW.READINGFC.CO.UK**
e:mail: **CUSTOMERSERVICE@READINGFC.CO.UK**
tel no: **0118 968 1100**
colours: **WHITE WITH BLUE HOOPS SHIRTS, WHITE SHORTS**
nickname: **THE ROYALS**
season 2009/10: **CHAMPIONSHIP**

Last Season: **4th** (p**46**; w**21**; d**14**; l**11**; gf**72**; ga**40**)

Relegated at the end of the 2007/08 season, it was widely expected that Steve Coppell's Reading side would feature in the battle for both the automatic promotion places and for the Play-Offs and, in this, fans were not to be disappointed. In the hunt for an automatic promotion place from the start of the season, by Christmas and following a run of five straight League wins, the Royals were a comfortable second behind ultimate champions Wolverhampton Wanderers. However, in a division where none of the top challengers excelled for the duration of the season, Reading's home form during the second half of the season was to prove the club's downfall. Two home wins and five defeats – including losses to struggling teams like Nottingham Forest – out of the last 11 home fixtures meant that Reading was one of three teams – along with Birmingham City and Sheffield United – capable of seizing second place. Sheffield's 0-0 draw at Crystal Palace means that the result at the Madejski Stadium was critical as Reading played host to City. A 2-1 victory for Birmingham consigned Reading to the Play-Offs. A 1-0 defeat at Burnley gave the Lancashire side the edge, which they added to with a 2-0 victory at Reading. Following the failure of his team to reach the Play-Off Final, Steve Coppell stood down as manager. New boss, Brendan Rodgers, will inherit a team capable of again reaching the Play-Offs at the very least but one which may well have lost a number of significant players over the close season.

Advance Tickets Tel No: 0844 249 1871
Fax: 0118 968 1101
Training Ground: Reading FC Academy Training Ground, Hogwood Lane, Arborfield Garrison, Wokingham RG40 4QW
Brief History: Founded 1871. Amalgamated with Reading Hornets in 1877 and with Earley in 1889. Former Grounds: Reading Recreation Ground, Reading Cricket Ground, Coley Park, Caversham Cricket Ground and Elm Park (1895-1998); moved to the Madejski Stadium at the start of the 1998/99 season. Founder-members of the Third Division in 1920. Record attendance (at Elm Park) 33,042; (at Madejski Stadium) 24,122
(Total) Current Capacity: 24,200 (all seated)
Visiting Supporters' Allocation: 4,500 (maximum in the Fosters Lager South Stand)
Nearest Railway Station: Reading (2.5 miles)
Parking (Car): 1,800-space car park at the ground, 700 of these spaces are reserved
Parking (Coach/Bus): As directed
Other Clubs Sharing Ground: London Irish RUFC
Police Force and Tel No: Thames Valley (0118 953 6000)
Disabled Visitors' Facilities:
Wheelchairs: 128 designated spaces on all four sides of the ground
Blind: 12 places for match day commentaries
Anticipated Development(s): The club applied for Planning Permission to expand the capacity of the Madejski Stadium by 14,000 seats in October 2005, taking the ground's capacity up from 24,000 to 38,000. Permission was subsequently granted and will involve extending the North, South and East stands. Work was scheduled to start in the summer of 2008 with an anticipated completion date of the end of 2009. Work has, however, yet to start on the ground's extension. A new station – Reading Green Park – on the line from Reading to Basingstoke is scheduled to open in early 2010 to serve the Green Park Business Park and the Madejski Stadium.

WEST (ULTIMA BUSINESS SOLUTIONS) STAND
UPPER
LOWER
PITCH SIZE
102 X 70 metres
SOUTH (FOSTERS LAGER) STAND
AWAY
NORTH (NPOWER) STAND
EAST (KYOCERA MITA) STAND
ACRE ROAD

C Club Offices
S Club Shop

1 North Stand
2 East Stand
3 South Stand (away)
4 West Stand
5 A33 Basingstoke Road
6 A33 to M4 (Jct 11)
7 A33 to Reading Town Centre
   and station (two miles)
8 Hurst Way
9 Boot End

↑ North direction (approx)

◄ 702329
▼ 702341

rochdale

Spotland Stadium, Willbutts Lane, Rochdale, OL11 5DS

website: **WWW.ROCHDALEAFC.CO.UK**
e:mail: **OFFICE@ROCHDALEAFC.CO.UK**
tel no: **0844 826 1907**
colours: **BLUE SHIRTS, BLUE SHORTS**
nickname: **THE DALE**
season 2009/10: **LEAGUE TWO**

Last Season: **6th** (p**46**; w**19**; d**13**; l**14**; gf**70**; ga**59**)

Beaten in the Play-Off Final at the end of the 2007/08 season, hopes were high at Spotland that in 2008/09 the club would finally be able to shed its record as the club to have played in the fourth tier of English football for the longest – it was in 1973/74 that the team was relegated from the old Third Division. A mediocre start to the campaign saw Rochdale mid-table initially but four straight League wins took Keith Hill's team into the Play-Off places in early November and the club remained one of the teams competing for the Play-offs for the remainder of the season. Finishing in sixth place – albeit a false spot given that both Rotherham and Darlington would have been higher had they not suffered a deduction in points – the Dale faced Gillingham in the Play-Offs. A 0-0 draw at Spotland handed the advantage to the Kent side and a 2-1 victory at Priestfield for the home side ensured that Rochdale will again be in League Two in 2009/10. For the new season Hill's team ought to again be one of those achieving the Play-Offs.

Advance Tickets Tel No: 0844 826 1907
Fax: 01706 648466
Training Ground: No specific facility
Brief History: Founded 1907 from former Rochdale Town F.C. (founded 1900). Founder-members Third Division North (1921). Record attendance 24,231
(Total) Current Capacity: 10,262; (8,342 seated)
Visiting Supporters' Allocation: 3,650 maximum (seated) in Willbutts Lane (Westrose Leisure) Stand
Nearest Railway Station: Rochdale
Parking (Car): Rear of ground
Parking (Coach/Bus): Rear of ground
Other Clubs Sharing Ground: Rochdale Hornets RLFC
Police Force and Tel No: Greater Manchester (0161 872 5050)
Disabled Visitors' Facilities:
Wheelchairs: Main, WMG and Willbutts Lane stands – disabled area
Blind: Commentary available
Anticipated Development(s): None following completion of Willbutts Lane Stand.

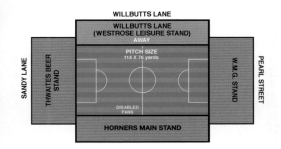

144

C Club Offices
S Club Shop
E Entrance(s) for visiting
supporters

1 Willbutts Lane
2 A627 Edenfield Road
3 Rochdale BR Station
(½ mile)
4 Sandy Lane
5 To M62
6 To M65 and North
7 WMG Stand
8 Willbutts Lane Stand

↑ *North direction (approx)*

◀ 701829
▼ 701848

rotherham united

Don Valley Stadium, Worksop Road, Sheffield, S9 3TL

website: **WWW.THEMILLERS.CO.UK**
e:mail: **OFFICE@ROTHERHAMUNITED.NET**
tel no: **0844 414 0733**
colours: **RED SHIRTS, WHITE SHORTS**
nickname: **THE MILLERS**
season 2009/10: **LEAGUE TWO**

Last Season*: **14th** (p**46**; w**21**; d**12**; l**13**; gf**60**; ga**46**)

Following the traumas of the close season in 2008, when the club faced relegation and Administration, the automatic deduction of 17 points and the enforced relocation from Millmoor to the Don Valley Stadium, events on the field proved that Mark Robins' team could compete effectively at this level. Indeed, had it not been for the loss of the points, United would have been amongst the teams in the Play-Off places. The team's potential was emphasised by the demolition of Championship side Southampton 3-1 at the Don Valley Stadium in the Third Round of the Carling Cup. Having started the season fearful that the points deduction would lead to a fight against relegation, the reality was that the team was always much stronger than the false position resulting from the deduction and, as a result, fans will be confident that, in 2009/10 the team will be undoubtedly one of these competing for automatic promotion.

Advance Tickets Tel No: 0844 414 0737
Fax: 0844 414 0744
Club Offices: Mangham House, Mangham Road, Barbot Hall Industrial Estate, Rotherham S61 4RJ
Training Ground: Hooton Training Ground, Thomas Street, Kilnhurst, Mexborough S64 5TF
Brief History: Founded 1877 (as Thornhill later Thornhill United), changed named to Rotherham County in 1905 and to Rotherham United in 1925 (amalgamated with Rotherham Town – Football League members 1893-97 – in 1925). Former Grounds include Red House Ground and Clifton Lane Cricket Ground, moved to Millmoor in 1907 and to the Don Valley Stadium in 2008. Record attendance (at Millmoor): 25,170; (at Don Valley Stadium) 5,404
(Total) Current Capacity: 25,000; however, only the partially-covered Main Stand is used for football with the three open sides unused
Visiting Supporters' Allocation: tbc
Nearest Railway Station: Arena/River Don Stadium stop on Sheffield Supertram network is 100m from the ground; Sheffield Supertram provides a link between the two nearest main line stations – Sheffield (two miles approx) and Meadowhall (1.5 miles approx)
Parking (Car): As directed
Parking (Coach/Bus): As directed
Other Clubs Sharing Ground: Sheffield Eagles RLFC
Police Force and Tel No: South Yorkshire (01709 371121)
Disabled Visitors' Facilities:
Wheelchairs: 12 wheelchair spaces
Blind: No special facility
Anticipated Development(s): Problems with occupation of the club's existing ground at Millmoor as a result of the process of bringing the club out of Administration and its acquisition by Tony Stewart led to the club leaving Millmoor during the summer of 2008 and relocating to the Don Valley Stadium. The club is hoping to work with Rotherham Council to develop a new community stadium in the town.

* 17 points deducted as a result of going into Administration in 2008

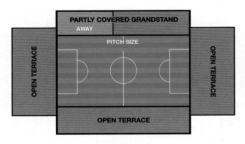

PARTLY COVERED GRANDSTAND
AWAY
PITCH SIZE
OPEN TERRACE
OPEN TERRACE
OPEN TERRACE

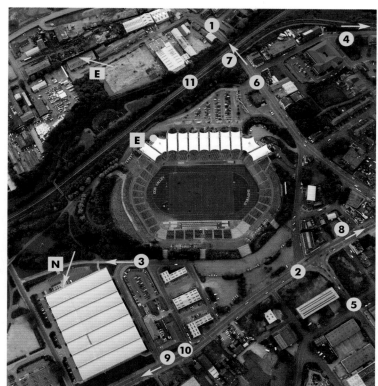

E Entrance(s) for visiting
supporters

1 B6085 Darnall Road
2 A6178 Attercliffe Road
3 To Arena/Don Valley Stadium
Supertram stop (one mile)
4 To Attercliffe Supertram stop
(one mile)
5 B6083 Newhall Road
6 Worksop Road
7 To A6012 and Darnall
railway station (two miles)
8 To Sheffield city centre and
main line railway station
(2½ miles)
9 To M1 Junction 34 (South)
(1½ miles)
10 To Rotherham town centre
(four miles)
11 Supertram route and freight-
only railway line

⬆ North direction (approx)

◀ 701360
▼ 701366

scunthorpe united

Glanford Park, Doncaster Road, Scunthorpe, DN15 8TD

website: **WWW.SCUNTHORPE–UNITED.CO.UK**
e:mail: **ADMIN@SCUNTHORPE–UNITED.CO.UK**
tel no: **0871 221 1899**
colours: **CLARET AND BLUE SHIRTS, CLARET SHORTS**
nickname: **THE IRON**
season 2009/10: **CHAMPIONSHIP**

Last Season: **6th** (promoted) (p**46**; w**22**; d**10**; l**14**; gf**82**; ga**63**)

Relegated at the end of the 2007/08 season, Nigel Adkins' team was one of those that at the start of the new campaign seemed to be on an express train back to the Championship with an impressive start to the season that saw the Iron top of the division at the end of October with nine wins and two draws from the club's first 13 League matches. Even as late as the end of January the club was still vying for one of the two automatic places but a run of five defeats in the next eight League matches saw the team slip out of even the Play-Off places and the club's fate was ultimately decided on the last day of the season when the Iron were home to Tranmere; an away win would ensure that Rovers finished sixth and thus pip United for the Play-Offs and, for much of the match, the result seemed to be going to in Tranmere's favour. However, an 88th minute equaliser ensured that Scunthorpe finished sixth. A 1-1 home draw against MK Dons in the Play-off Semi-Finals allied to a 0-0 draw away resulted in the tie being settled on penalties, which Scunthorpe won 7-6 to set up a Wembley final against Millwall. In the spring sunshine, Scunthorpe triumphed 3-2, coming from 2-1 down at half time with two late goals, to achieve an immediate return to the Championship. The team's last sojourn in the Championship lasted but one season and it's hard to escape the conclusion that Adkins and his team will face an uphill struggle if the Iron isn't to make an immediate return to League One.

Advance Tickets Tel No: 0871 221 1899

Fax: 01724 857986

Training Ground: Grange Farm, Neap House Road, Gunness, Scunthorpe DN15 8TX

Brief History: Founded 1899 as Scunthorpe United, amalgamated with North Lindsey to become 'Scunthorpe & Lindsey United' in 1912. Changed name to Scunthorpe United in 1956. Former Grounds: Crosby (Lindsey United) and Old Showground, moved to Glanford Park in 1988. Elected to Football League in 1950. Record attendance 8,906 (23,935 at Old Showground).

(Total) Current Capacity: 9,200; (6,400 seated)

Visiting Supporters' Allocation: 1,678 (all seated) in AMS (South) Stand

Nearest Railway Station: Scunthorpe

Parking (Car): At ground

Parking (Coach/Bus): At ground

Police Force and Tel No: Humberside (01724 282888)

Disabled Visitors' Facilities:

Wheelchairs: Grove Wharf Stand

Blind: Commentary available

Anticipated Development(s): The club is seeking planning permission to redevelop the North (Study United) Stand at Glanford Park with the intention of increasing the ground's capacity to 11,000. If consent is granted work should start during 2008. In addition, the club is also looking at the possibility of a further relocation, although nothing is confirmed at the present time.

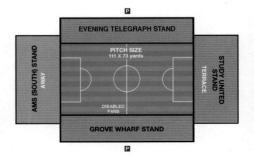

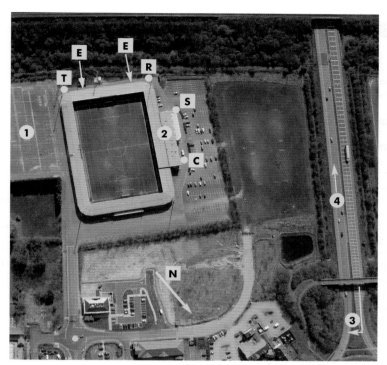

C Club Offices
S Club Shop
E Entrance(s) for visiting supporters
R Refreshment bars for visiting supporters
T Toilets for visiting supporters

1 Car Park
2 Evening Telegraph Stand
3 A18 to Scunthorpe BR Station and Town Centre (1½ miles)
4 M181 and M180 Junction 3

↑ North direction (approx)

◄ 700699
▼ 700707

sheffield united

Bramall Lane, Sheffield, S2 4SU

website: **WWW.SUFC.CO.UK**
e:mail: **INFO@SUFC.CO.UK**
tel no: **0871 222 1899**
colours: **RED AND WHITE STRIPED SHIRTS, BLACK SHORTS**
nickname: **THE BLADES**
season 2009/10: **CHAMPIONSHIP**

Last Season: **3rd** (p**46**; w**22**; d**14**; l**10**; gf**64**; ga**39**)

In the Blades' second season back in the Championship following the team's controversial relegation at the end of the 2006/07 season, Kevin Blackwell's team started slowly but as the season wore on became serious challengers for one of the two automatic promotion places and the club's fate was not settled until the ultimate game of the League season. Needing to better Birmingham City's result at Reading, Sheffield United faced a tricky away match at Crystal Palace – ironically a team managed by ex-Blades' boss Neil Warnock – but City's 2-1 victory at the Madejski Stadium made any result from Selhurst Park irrelevant – the Blades in fact drew 0-0 – and consigned United to the Play-Offs against Preston North End. A 1-1 draw away gave United the edge, which was duly built upon with a 1-0 home win at Bramall Lane to set up a final against Burnley at Wembley. Unfortunately, a 1-0 victory for the Lancashire side sent the Clarets up and left United again facing a season in the Championship. For the club's third season at this level, the two-year Premier League parachute payments will cease and, as other ex-Premier League teams have discovered, the disappearance of this cushion can lead to a struggle in the future. United ought to be one of the teams again vying for the Play-Offs at least but, with Blackwell's position in doubt after the Wembley defeat, there is some uncertainty as to the future at Bramall Lane.

Advance Tickets Tel No: 0871 222 1899
Fax: 0871 663 2430
Training Ground: The Hallam FM Academy @ Sheffield United, 614A Firshill Crescent, Sheffield S4 7DJ
Brief History: Founded 1889. (Sheffield Wednesday occasionally used Bramall Lane c1880.) Founder-members 2nd Division (1892). Record attendance 68,287
(Total) Current Capacity: 32,702 (all seated)
Visiting Supporters' Allocation: 3,000 (seated) can be increased to 5,200 if needed in Halliwells (Bramall Lane) Stand
Nearest Railway Station: Sheffield Midland
Parking (Car): Street parking
Parking (Coach/Bus): As directed by Police
Police Force and Tel No: South Yorkshire (0114 276 8522)
Disabled Visitors' Facilities:
Wheelchairs: South Stand
Blind: Commentary available
Anticipated Development(s): In late 2008 it was announced that the club was seeking planning permission to add 3,200 seats to the Bramall Lane Stand and replace its existing roof with a cantilevered structure. This work would increase the ground's capacity to 36,000 and the club has plans to take this to 40,000 with the redevelopment of the South stand. In January 2009 the Copthorne Hotel, sited behind the Westfield Stand, was opened.

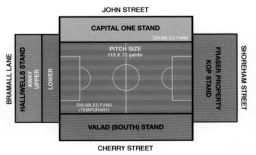

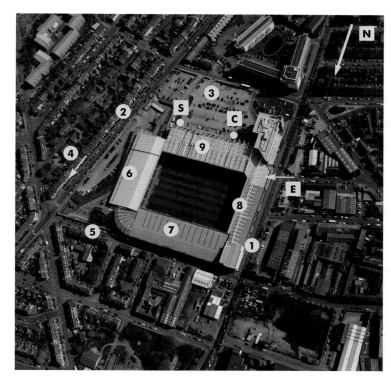

C Club Offices
S Club Shop
E Entrance(s) for visiting
  supporters

1 A621 Bramall Lane
2 Shoreham Street
3 Car Park
4 Sheffield Midland BR Station
  (¼ mile)
5 John Street
6 Hallam FM (Kop) Stand
7 John Street Stand
8 Bramall Lane
  (Gordon Lamb) Stand
9 Laver (South) Stand

↑ *North direction (approx)*

◀ 702290
▼ 702307

sheffield wednesday

Hillsborough, Sheffield, S6 1SW

website: **WWW.SWFC.CO.UK**
e:mail: **ENQUIRIES@SWFC.CO.UK**
tel no: **0871 995 1867**
colours: **BLUE AND WHITE STRIPED SHIRTS, BLACK SHORTS**
nickname: **THE OWLS**
season 2009/10: **CHAMPIONSHIP**

Last Season: **12th** (p**46**; w**16**; d**13**; l**17**; gf**51**; ga**58**)

Now established as a mid-table team in the Championship after four seasons at this level, Brian Laws' Sheffield Wednesday initially looked as though it might struggle in 2008/09 when, having had a promising start to the season which saw the Owls reach fifth place and a possible Play-Off place following a 1-0 victory at home against in the Sheffield Derby, a run of five defeats in seven games saw the team gradually drift down the table. From then on the team seemed destined to achieve the position of mid-table mediocrity that was the ultimate result. Outside the League, the Owls made their first ever visit to the Don Valley Stadium – the new home of neighbours Rotherham United – for a replay of a Carling Cup First Round match; with the match tied after extra time, the home side won 5-3 on penalties. Laws has been boss at Hillsborough now for almost three years; he has ensured that Wednesday are now firmly established in the Championship. For 2009/10 fans will be hoping that he has the ability to see the team push more consistently towards the Play-Offs; in this he will be aided by Howard Wilkinson, who returned to the club in an advisory role in January.

Advance Tickets Tel No: 0870 900 1867
Fax: 0114 221 2122
Training Ground: Sheffield Wednesday Football Club Training Ground, Middlewood Road, Sheffield, S6 4HA
Brief History: Founded 1867 as The Wednesday F.C. (changed to Sheffield Wednesday c1930). Former Grounds: London Road, Wyrtle Road (Heeley), Sheaf House Ground, Encliffe & Olive Grove (Bramall Lane also used occasionally), moved to Hillsborough (then named 'Owlerton') in 1899. Founder-members Second Division (1892). Record attendance 72,841.
(Total) Current Capacity: 39,812 (all seated)
Visiting Supporters' Allocation: 3,700 (all seated) in West Stand Upper
Nearest Railway Station: Sheffield (2 miles)
Parking (Car): Street Parking
Parking (Coach/Bus): Owlerton Stadium
Police Force and Tel No: South Yorkshire (0114 276 8522)
Disabled Visitors' Facilities:
Wheelchairs: North and Lower West Stands
Blind: Commentary available

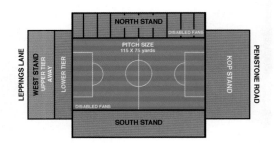

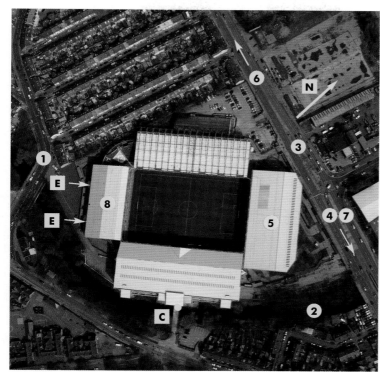

C Club Offices
E Entrance(s) for visiting
  supporters

1 Leppings Lane
2 River Don
3 A61 Penistone Road North
4 Sheffield BR Station and
  City Centre (2 miles)
5 Spion Kop
6 To M1 (North)
7 To M1 (South)
8 West Stand

↑ North direction (approx)

◄ 701078
▼ 701082

shrewsbury town

The ProStar Stadium, Oteley Road, Shrewsbury, SY2 6ST

website: **WWW.SHREWSBURYTOWN.COM**
e:mail: **IAN@SHREWSBURYTOWN.CO.UK**
tel no: **0871 811 8800**
colours: **BLUE SHIRTS, BLUE SHORTS**
nickname: **THE SHREWS**
season 2009/10: **LEAGUE TWO**

Last Season: **7th** (p**46**; w**17**; d**18**; l**11**; gf**61**: ga**44**)

Ultimately a disappointing season for Paul Simpson's Shrewsbury Town as, for the second season in three, the Shrews were beaten in the League Two Play-Off Final at Wembley – this time by Gillingham with the only goal of the match being scored in the 90th minute. In a sense, however, Town were only in the Play-offs as a result of the fact that both Darlington and Rotherham would have been higher had they not suffered point deductions for going into Administration. As it was, Shrewsbury's home form was excellent but the team struggled away from the ProStar Stadium, winning only three times on its travels – including a last-day victory away at Play-Off rivals Dagenham & Redbridge, a result that allowed Shrewsbury to pip the London team for the all-important seventh place when all the Daggers required was a draw. In the Play-Off Semi-Finals the team lost the home leg to Bury 1-0 following an embarrassing own goal but had triumphed 1-0 after extra time at Gigg Lane and won through on penalties to face Gillingham in the Final courtesy of heroics from on-loan goalkeeper Luke Daniels. Away from the League, the club's poor away form was also reflected in an early exit from the FA Cup when the team went down 3-1 away at non-League Blyth Spartans in the First Round. The last time that Town lost in a Play-Off final, the following season proved more of a struggle but fans will be hoping that history doesn't repeat itself. Provided that Simpson can build upon the core of the team that went to Wembley, the Shrews should once again prove to be contenders for the Play-Offs at least.

Advance Tickets Tel No: 01743 273943
Fax: 0871 811 8801
Training Ground: Sundorne castle training Ground, Newport Road, Sundorne, Shrewsbury SY1 4RR
Brief History: Founded 1886. Former Grounds: Monkmoor Racecourse, Ambler's Field; The Barracks Ground and the Gay Meadow (1910-2007); moved to the new ground for start of 2007/08 season. Elected to Football League 1950; relegated to Nationwide Conference at end of 2002/03 and promoted back to the Football League, via the Play-Offs, at the end of 2003/04. Record attendance at the Gay Meadow 18,917; at the New Stadium 8,753
(Total) Current Capacity: 9,875 (all seated)
Visiting Supporters' Allocation: tbc (North Stand)
Nearest Railway Station: Shrewsbury (two miles)
Parking (Car): at ground
Parking (Coach/Bus): at ground
Police Force and Tel No: West Mercia (01743 232888)
Disabled Visitors' Facilities:
Wheelchairs: c40 spaces in North (away), South and East stands
Blind: Commentary available
Anticipated Development(s): The ground was originally designed to permit the construction of corner infill accommodation to take the ground's total capacity to 12,500. Work on this development was scheduled to start in the summer of 2009.

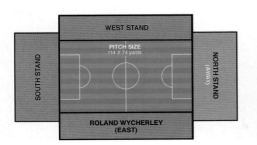

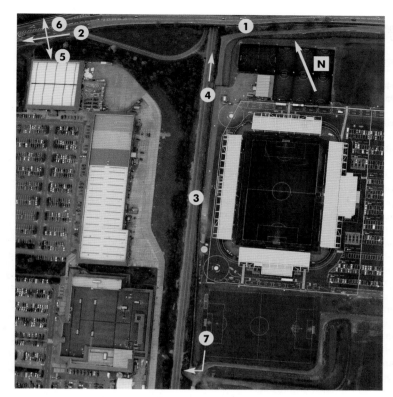

1 B4380 Oteley Road
2 Meole Brace roundabout
3 Shrewsbury-Hereford railway line
4 To Shrewsbury station (two miles)
5 A5112 Hereford Road to A5 (ring road)
6 A5191 Hereford Road to town centre and railway station
7 Footpath under railway to retail park

↑ North direction (approx)

◀ 701114
▼ 701118

southampton

St Mary's Stadium, Britannia Road, Southampton, SO14 5FP

website: **WWW.SAINTSFC.CO.UK**
e:mail: **SFC@SAINTSFC.CO.UK**
tel no: **0845 688 9448**
colours: **RED AND WHITE SHIRTS, BLACK SHORTS**
nickname: **THE SAINTS**
season 2009/10: **LEAGUE ONE**

Last Season: **23rd** (Relegated) (p**46**; w**10**; d**15**; l**21**; gf**46**; ga**69**)

A troubled season for the Saints both on and off the field saw the club's holding company collapse into Administration just before the end of the season and the team relegated to League One following the home draw with Burnley in the penultimate game of the season. Relegated to the third tier of English football for the first time since promotion at the end of the 1959/60 season, Saints join two other ex-Premier League outfits – Charlton and Norwich – in the drop. The season started with Dutchman Jan Poortvliet in charge; he had been appointed towards the end of the 2007/08 season but his reign in charge at St Mary's Stadium was destined to last only eight months before he departed at the end of January following a run of results that had left the team deep in the relegation mire. The club's financial position and the loss of key players as a result had weakened the team and results under Poortvliet's successor, fellow Dutchman Mark Wotte, did not significantly improve. Away from the League, the club suffered a 3-1 defeat away at Rotherham in the Third Round of the Carling Cup. In terms of the club's potential in League One, much will depend upon how quickly a deal is put in place and how the head coach – now Alan Pardew following the take-over of the club by a new consortium and the departure of Wotte – is able to mould a squad for League One. Potentially, a Play-Off place but other ex-Premier League teams have struggled at this level – and that was without the disbenefit of an Administration and a 10-point deduction.

Advance Tickets Tel No: 0845 688 9288
Fax: 0845 688 9445
Training Ground: Staplewood, Club House, Long Lane, Marchwood, Southampton SO40 4WR
Brief History: Founded 1885 as 'Southampton St. Mary's Young Men's Association (changed name to Southampton in 1897). Former Grounds: Northlands Road, Antelope Ground, County Ground, moved to The Dell in 1898 and to St Mary's Stadium in 2001. Founder members Third Division (1920). Record attendance (at The Dell) 31,044; (at St Mary's) 32,151
(Total) Current Capacity: 32,689 (all seated)
Visiting Supporters' Allocation: c3,200 in Northam Stand (can be increased to 4,750 if required)
Nearest Railway Station: Southampton Central
Parking (Car): Street parking or town centre car parks
Parking (Coach/Bus): As directed by the police
Police Force and Tel No: Hampshire (02380 335444)
Disabled Visitors' Facilities:
Wheelchairs: c200 places
Blind: Commentary available
Anticipated Development(s): Following completion of the new stadium the club has no further plans at present.

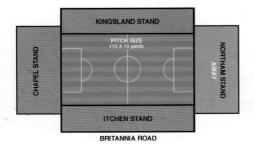

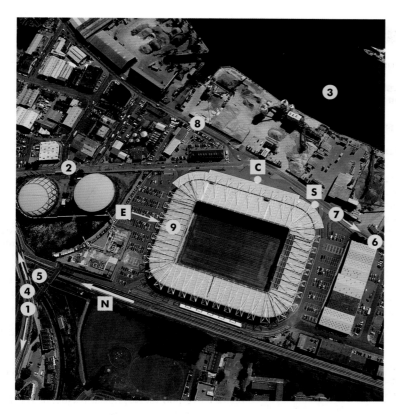

C Club Offices
S Club Shop
E Entrance(s) for visiting
  supporters

1 A3024 Northam Road
2 B3028 Britannia Road
3 River Itchen
4 To M27 (five miles)
5 To Southampton Central
  station and town centre
6 Marine Parade
7 To A3025 (and Itchen
  toll bridge)
8 Belvedere Road
9 Northam Stand

⬆ North direction (approx)

◄ 699202
▼ 699209

southend united

Roots Hall Ground, Victoria Avenue, Southend-on-Sea, SS2 6NQ

website: **WWW.SOUTHENDUNITED.CO.UK**
e:mail: **INFO@SOUTHEND-UNITED.CO.UK**
tel no: **01702 304050**
colours: **BLUE SHIRTS, BLUE SHORTS**
nickname: **THE SHRIMPERS**
season 2009/10: **LEAGUE ONE**

Last Season: **8th** (p**46**; w**21**; d**8**; l**17**; gf**58**; ga**61**)

Having made the Play-offs at the end of the 2007/08 season, hopes were high that Steve Tilson's team would once again feature in the League One promotion race but a poor start to the season saw the club in the relegation zone after five matches although the team's form slightly improved thereafter. However, at the end of January the Shrimpers were still languishing in 17th place but a run of 12 victories in 16 League matches dragged the team up to eighth by the middle of April – the run coming just too late to see the team achieve a Play-Off place, however. With the new season possibly the last to be played at Roots Hall – the club's home for more than 50 years – expectations will be high that Tilson's team can achieve the Play-Offs at least. With three ex-Premier League teams relegated in 2008/09 to League One and a number of other ambitious teams already operating at this level, United may struggle but, provided the team can replicate the late-season form from last year then the Play-Offs ought to be a realistic target.

Advance Tickets Tel No: 0844 477 0077
Fax: 01702 304124
Training Ground: Eastern Avenue, Southend-on-Sea SS2 4DX
Brief History: Founded 1906. Former Grounds: Roots Hall, Kursaal, the Stadium Grainger Road, moved to Roots Hall (new Ground) 1955. Founder-members Third Division (1920). Record attendance 31,033
(Total) Current Capacity: 12,392 (all seated)
Visiting Supporters' Allocation: 2,000 (maximum) (all seated) in North Stand and North West Enclosure
Nearest Railway Station: Prittlewell
Parking (Car): Street parking
Parking (Coach/Bus): Car park at Ground
Police Force and Tel No: Essex (01702 431212)
Disabled Visitors' Facilities:
Wheelchairs: West Stand
Blind: Commentary available
Anticipated Development(s): The club submitted a proposal for the construction of its new £25 million 22,000-seat ground at Fossetts Farm to the council in early October 2006 and formal consent was granted by the council in January 2007 although this was subject to a public inquiry. Formal approval for the work was granted in March 2008. The new ground, designed by HOK (who also designed the Emirates Stadium), is scheduled for completion by the start of the 2010/11 season. A further complication is that planning permission for the redevelopment of Roots Hall is still outstanding. Final consent for the new ground was given by the government in July 2008. Funding for the work will come in part from the sale of Roots Hall to Sainsbury's for the construction of a new supermarket.

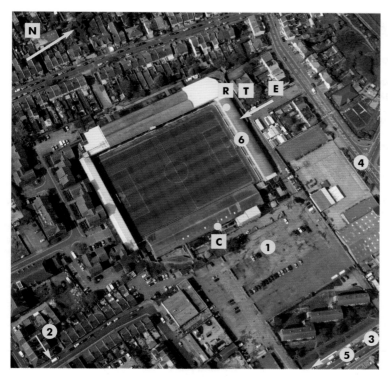

C Club Offices
E Entrance(s) for visiting supporters
R Refreshment bars for visiting supporters
T Toilets for visiting supporters

1 Director's Car Park
2 Prittlewell BR Station (¼ mile)
3 A127 Victoria Aveneue
4 Fairfax Drive
5 Southend centre (½ mile)
6 North (Universal Cycles) Stand

↑ North direction (approx)

◄ 702417
▼ 702451

stockport county

Edgeley Park, Hardcastle Road, Edgeley, Stockport, SK3 9DD

website: **WWW.STOCKPORTCOUNTY.COM**
e:mail: **FANS@STOCKPORTCOUNTY.COM**
tel no: **0161 286 8888**
colours: **BLUE AND WHITE STRIPE SHIRTS, BLUE SHORTS**
nickname: **THE HATTERS**
season 2009/10: **LEAGUE ONE**

Last Season*: **18th** (p**46**; w**16**; d**12**; l**18**; gf**59**; ga**57**)

A mediocre season on the field saw Jim Gannon's County theoretically achieve a position of mid-table security but the decision, towards the end of the season, to put the club into Administration saw an automatic 10-point deduction, which saw the club move effectively from 14th place to 18th. In reality, however, that was the least of the fans' worries as a greater concern was whether the team would survive to start the 2009/10 season at all. As the Administrators took action – one of their first decisions was to make the popular and successful Jim Gannon redundant along with assistant Peter Ward – there was concern amongst the fans as to what the result of the process might be. In the past League clubs have gone into Administration and have survived – although it has occasionally been a close-run thing – and, for the 2009/10 season, County fans will be hoping that their team perpetuates this history. Trying to rebuild a squad during the close season whilst under Administration can be difficult and the realistic expectations for the new campaign must be that the team will struggle to survive in League One under new manager Gary Ablett; the reality is, however, that for fans for the club to survive will perhaps be a triumph in its own right.

Advance Tickets Tel No: 0845 688 5799
Fax: 0161 429 7392
Training Ground: Details omitted at club's request
Brief History: Founded 1883 as Heaton Norris Rovers, changed name to Stockport County in 1890. Former Grounds: Heaton Norris Recreation Ground, Heaton Norris Wanderers Cricket Ground, Chorlton's Farm, Ash Inn Ground, Wilkes Field (Belmont Street) and Nursery Inn (Green Lane), moved to Edgeley Park in 1902. Record attendance 27,833
(Total) Current Capacity: 10,650 (all seated)
Visiting Supporters' Allocation: 1,558 (all-seated) on the open Railway End plus 800 seats, if required, on Popular Side
Nearest Railway Station: Stockport
Parking (Car): Street Parking
Parking (Coach/Bus): As directed by Police
Other Clubs Sharing Ground: Sale Sharks RUFC
Police Force and Tel No: Greater Manchester (0161 872 5050)
Disabled Visitors' Facilities:
Wheelchairs: Main and Cheadle stands
Blind: Headsets available
Anticipated Development(s): Although the club is still planning for the reconstruction of the Railway End, with the intention of constructing a new 5,500-seat capacity stand on the site, there is no time scale for this work (which had originally been planned for 1999/2000). Theoretically, the next phase after the Railway End would be an upgrade to the Vernon BS Stand, with the intention of making the ground's capacity 20,000.

*10 points deducted as a result of going into Administration in 2009

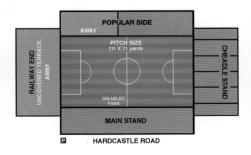

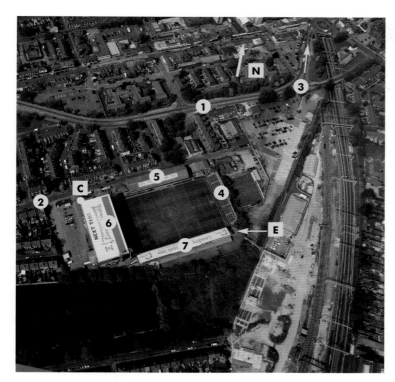

C Club Offices
E Entrance(s) for visiting supporters

1 Mercian Way
2 Hardcastle Road
3 Stockport BR station (¼ mile)
4 Railway End
5 Main Stand
6 Cheadle Stand
7 Vernon BS Stand

↑ *North direction (approx)*

◄ 701279
▼ 701273

stoke city

Britannia Stadium, Stanley Matthews Way, Stoke-on-Trent, ST4 4EG

website: **WWW.STOKECITYFC.COM**
e:mail: **INFO@STOKECITYFC.COM**
tel no: **0871 663 2008**
colours: **RED AND WHITE STRIPED SHIRTS, WHITE SHORTS**
nickname: **THE POTTERS**
season 2009/10: **PREMIER LEAGUE**

Last Season: **12th** (p**38**; w**12**; d**9**; l**17**; gf**38**; ga**55**)

Promoted at the end of the 2007/08 season, Stoke City had two primary aims: to finish in at least 17th place and to secure a greater points total than the club achieved when last in the top division in the mid-1980s. Initially the prognosis did not look good as the team struggled to make an impact. In early October, with only one win in the club's first seven League matches, Stoke was firmly rooted in the relegation zone and a later run of 11 matches without a win – including defeats at home 1-0 to Derby County in the Quarter-Finals of the Carling Cup and 2-0 away at League One Hartlepool in the Third Round of the FA Cup – seemed to confirm that the Potters' stay in the Premier League would be short. In the club's first 23 League matches a total of 21 points had been secured; in the next 15, however, no fewer than 24 points were achieved with the result that Tony Pulis's team finished in a comfortable mid-table position. Of the points achieved, no fewer than 35 were gained at home. For 2009/10 the challenge will be to build upon this success. Other clubs have suffered severely in their second season at this level and Pulis is an astute enough operator to realise that the job is only half done thus far. He'll be looking to strengthen the squad significantly during the close season and he'll need to do so if Stoke are not to suffer from second-seasonitis. Playing teams for the first time at this level for some years, Stoke had the benefit of being unfamiliar; sticking to the same tactics in the second season may be counterproductive. Given the circumstances, it's likely that City will again struggle to retain a Premier League position in 2009/10.

Advance Tickets Tel No: 0871 663 2007
Fax: 01782 592 210
Training Ground: Michelin Sports Ground, Rose Tree Avenue, Trent Vale, Stoke On Trent, ST4 6NL
Brief History: Founded 1863 as Stoke F.C., amalgamated with Stoke Victoria in 1878, changed to Stoke City in 1925. Former Grounds: Sweetings Field, Victoria Ground (1878-1997), moved to new ground for start of 1997/98 season. Record attendance (at Victoria Ground): 51,380; at Britannia Stadium 28,218
(Total) Current Capacity: 28,383 (all seated)
Visiting Supporters' Allocation: 2,800 (in the South Stand)
Nearest Railway Station: Stoke-on-Trent
Parking (Car): The 650 parking spaces at the ground are for officials and guests only. The 1,600 spaces in the South car park are pre-booked only, with the majority held by season ticket holders. There is some on-street parking, but with a 10-15min walk.
Parking (Coach/Bus): As directed
Police Force and Tel No: Staffordshire (01782 744644)
Disabled Visitors' Facilities:
Wheelchairs: 164 places for disabled spectators
Blind: Commentaries available
Anticipated Development(s): There are long-term plans to increase the ground's capacity to 30,000 by the construction of a corner stand between the John Smith Stand and the Boothen End but there is no timescale for this work.

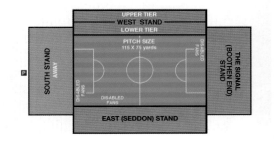

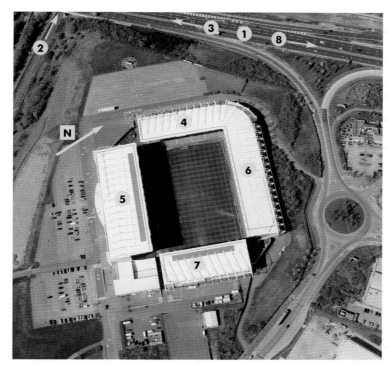

1 A50
2 To Stoke BR station
3 To A500 Queensway and City Centre, railway station and M6
4 North Stand
5 West Stand
6 East Stand
7 South Stand (away)
8 To Uttoxeter

⬆ North direction (approx)

◀ 700729
▼ 700734

sunderland

Stadium of Light, Sunderland SR5 1SU

website: **WWW.SAFC.COM**
e:mail: **ENQUIRIES@SAFC.COM**
tel no: **0871 911 1200**
colours: **RED AND WHITE STRIPED SHIRTS, BLACK SHORTS**
nickname: **THE BLACK CATS**
season 2009/10: **PREMIER LEAGUE**

Last Season: **16th** (p**38**; w**9** d**0**; l**20**; gf**34**; ga**54**)

In early December, following a run of five defeats in six games that left the Black Cats in 18th place in the Premier League and facing an uphill battle to retain the club's Premier League place, Roy Keane departed as manager after just over two years in the position. He was replaced by Ricky Sbragia. Under Sbragia, the club's form picked up and by the beginning of February the club had moved up to mid-table. However, a late loss of form, which saw the team win only one of the next 12 League matches saw the Black Cats drawn back down towards the drop zone and, in theory, still mathematically capable of being relegated on the last day (although this required Sunderland to lose and both Hull City and Newcastle United to win). In the event, Sunderland's 3-2 defeat at home to Chelsea was not to lead to the drop as both Hull and Newcastle lost as well. Immediately after the match it was announced that Sbragia was standing down as manager; the new manager, Steve Bruce, will face the challenge of recruiting players to the Stadium of Light and building a squad capable of surviving another season at this level. The teams promoted from the Championship at the end of 2008/09 look potentially stronger than those that came up at the end of 2007/08 and so a number of existing Premier League teams – of which Sunderland may well be one – may struggle to survive come the end of May 2010.

Advance Tickets Tel No: 0871 911 1973
Fax: 0191 551 5123
Training Ground: The Academy of Light, Sunderland Road, Sunderland SR6 7UN
Brief History: Founded 1879 as 'Sunderland & District Teachers Association', changed to 'Sunderland Association' in 1880 and shortly after to 'Sunderland'. Former Grounds: Blue House Field, Groves Field (Ashbrooke), Horatio Street, Abbs Field, Newcastle Road and Roker Park (1898-1997); moved to Stadium of Light for the start of the 1997/98 season. Record crowd (at Roker Park): 75,118; (at Stadium of Light) 48,353
(Total) Current Capacity: 49,000 (all seated)
Visiting Supporters' Allocation: 3,000 (South Stand)
Nearest Railway Station: Stadium of Light (Tyne & Wear Metro)
Parking (Car): Car park at ground reserved for season ticket holders. Limited on-street parking (but the police may decide to introduce restrictions). Otherwise off-street parking in city centre
Parking (Coach/Bus): As directed
Police Force and Tel No: Tyne & Wear (0191 510 2020)
Disabled Visitors' Facilities:
Wheelchairs: 180 spots
Blind: Commentary available
Anticipated Development(s): The club has planning permission to increase capacity at the Stadium of Light by 7,200 in an expanded Metro FM Stand and plans a further 9,000 in a second tier to the McEwans Stand, taking the ultimate capacity of the ground to 64,000. There is, however, no confirmed timescale.

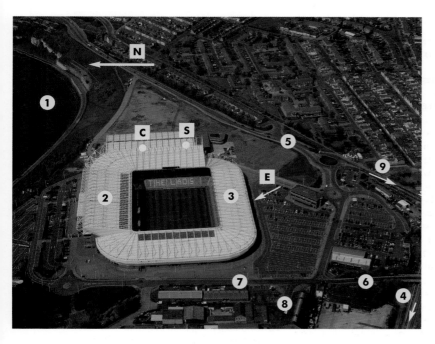

C   Club Offices
S   Club Shop
E   Entrance(s) for visiting
    supporters

1   River Wear
2   North (McEwans) Stand
3   South (Metro FM) Stand
    (away)
4   To Sunderland BR station
    (¹/₂ mile)
5   Southwick Road
6   Stadium Way
7   Millennium Way
8   Hay Street
9   To Wearmouth Bridge (via
    A1018 North Bridge Street)
    to City Centre

↑   North direction (approx)

◄ 701290
▼ 701284

swansea city

Liberty Stadium, Morfa, Swansea SA1 2FA

website: **WWW.SWANSEACITY.NET**
e:mail: **INFO@SWANSEACITYFC.CO.UK**
tel no: **01792 616600**
colours: **WHITE SHIRTS, WHITE SHORTS**
nickname: **THE SWANS**
season 2009/10: **CHAMPIONSHIP**

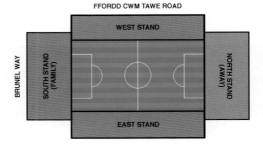

Last Season: **8th** (p**46**; w**16**; d**20**; l**10**; gf**63**; ga**50**)

Promoted at the end of the 2007/08 season into the Championship, Roberto Martinez's team proved itself to be the division's dark horse although a poorish start to the campaign, which saw the Swans languishing in 18th position after eight League matches, suggested that relegation rather than promotion was the more likely result. By mid-November, however, the club had reached an impressive seventh place but then a run of eight draws and a defeat in the next nine League matches saw the team drift back down the table. This sequence was then followed by six wins and two draws in the next eight matches so that by early February seventh spot was again held. Thereafter, the Swans remained in the hunt for the Play-Offs but remained dogged by inconsistent form so that the all-important sixth place remained elusive. During the close season Martinez departed to take over at Wigan, with ex-QPR boss Paulo Sousa appointed to replace him. For 2009/10, provided that club can avoid a severe bout of second-seasonitis, the Swans should, once again, have the potential for a good top-half finish and an outside chance of the Play-offs but greater consistency will be needed if this is to be achieved.

Advance Tickets Tel No: 0870 400004
Fax: 01792 616606
Training Ground: Llandarcy Academy of Sport, Neath SA10 6JD
Brief History: Founded 1900 as Swansea Town, changed to Swansea City in 1970. Former grounds: various, including Recreation Ground, and Vetch Field (1912-2005); moved to the new ground for the start of the 2005/06 season. Founder-members Third Division (1920). Record attendance (at Vetch Field): 32,796; (at Liberty Stadium) 19,288.
(Total) Current Capacity: 20,500 (all seated)
Visiting Supporters' Allocation: 3,500 maximum in North Stand
Nearest Railway Station: Swansea
Parking (Car): Adjacent to ground
Parking (Coach/Bus): As directed
Other Clubs Sharing Ground: Swansea Ospreys RUFC
Police Force and Tel No: South Wales (01792 456999)
Disabled Visitors' Facilities:
Wheelchairs: 252 spaces
Blind: no special facility
Anticipated Development(s): After several years of uncertainty, Swansea City relocated to the new White Rock Stadium with its 20,000 all-seater capacity for the start of the 2005/06 season. The ground, which cost £27 million to construct and which was built near the site of the old Morfa stadium, is shared by the Swansea Ospreys RUFC team.

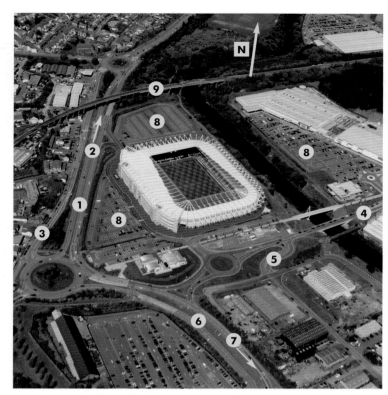

1 A4067 Ffordd Cwm Tawe Road
2 A4067 to A48 and M4 Junction 44 (five miles)
3 B4603 Neath Road
4 Brunel Way
5 Normandy Road
6 A4217
7 To Swansea city centre and BR railway station (two miles)
8 Parking
9 Cardiff-Swansea railway line

⬆ North direction (approx)

◀ 700168
▼ 700180

swindon town

County Ground, County Road, Swindon, SN1 2ED

website: **WWW.SWINDONTOWNFC.CO.UK**
e:mail: **ENQUIRIES@SWINDONTOWNFC.CO.UK**
tel no: **0871 423 6433**
colours: **RED SHIRTS, WHITE SHORTS**
nickname: **THE ROBINS**
season 2009/10: **LEAGUE ONE**

Last Season: **15th** (p**46**; w**12**; d**17**; l**17**; gf**68**; ga**71**)

Following a disappointing start to the League campaign, with Town winning only four out of 14 League matches to stand in 17th place in League One and defeats in the FA Cup – embarrassingly 1-0 away at non-League Histon – and in the Associate Members' Cup – 2-0 away at Brighton – Maurice Malpas departed as manager in mid-November after less than a year in charge. Initially he was replaced by Dave Byrne as caretaker boss but the club appointed the experienced Danny Wilson to the County Ground hot-seat at the end of November. Under Wilson, the club's form was variable and there was a significant chance that the club faced relegation as it gradually drifted down the League One table; in mid-March following a 1-0 defeat at Elland Road, the club stood in 21st place. However, a run of five wins and three draws in the club's final 10 League games was enough to drag the team to a position of mid-table safety. With Wilson planning a wholesale revamping of the squad for 2009/10, Town should be able to build upon his wide managerial experience but perhaps a top-half finish is perhaps the best that can be hoped for.

Advance Tickets Tel No: 0871 223 2300
Fax: 0844 880 1112
Training Ground: Zurich, Wanborough, Swindon SN4 0DY
Brief History: Founded 1881. Former Grounds: Quarry Ground, Globe Road, Croft Ground, County Ground (adjacent to current Ground and now Cricket Ground), moved to current County Ground in 1896. Founder-members Third Division (1920). Record attendance 32,000
(Total) Current Capacity: 15,700 (all seated)
Visiting Supporters' Allocation: 3,342 (all seated) maximum in Arkell's Stand and Stratton Bank (open)
Nearest Railway Station: Swindon
Parking (Car): Town Centre
Parking (Coach/Bus): Adjacent car park
Police Force and Tel No: Wiltshire (01793 528111)
Disabled Visitors' Facilities:
Wheelchairs: In front of Arkell's Stand
Blind: Commentary available
Anticipated Development(s): In late 2008 Town's chairman announced that the club would now seek to redevelop the County Ground rather than relocate.

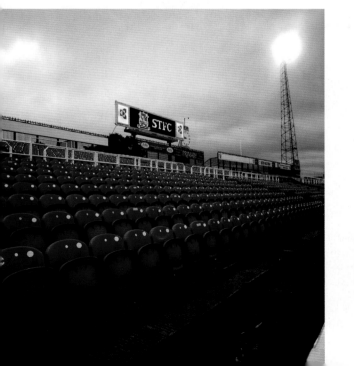

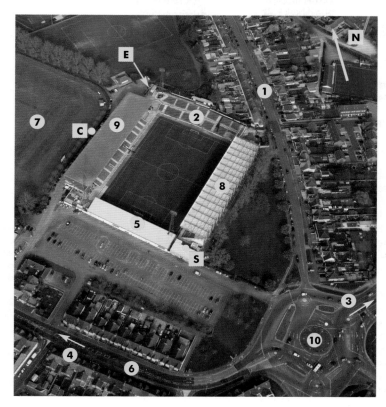

N

C Club Offices
S Club Shop
E Entrance(s) for visiting
   supporters

1 Shrivenham Road
2 Stratton Bank (away)
3 A345 Queens Drive
   (M4 Junction 15 –
   3½ miles)
4 Swindon BR Station
   (½ mile)
5 Town End
6 Car Park
7 County Cricket Ground
8 South Stand
9 Arkell's Stand
10 'Magic' Roundabout

↑ North direction (approx)

◄ 702352
▾ 702372

torquay united

Plainmoor, Torquay TQ1 3PS

Web Site: **WWW.TORQUAYUNITED.COM**
E-mail: **RECEPTION@TORQUAYUNITED.COM**
Telephone: **01803 328666**
Club Colours: **YELLOW AND BLUE SHIRTS, YELLOW SHORTS**
Nickname: **THE GULLS**
League: **LEAGUE TWO**

Last Season: **4th** (promoted) (p**46**; w**23**; d**14**; l**9**; gf**72**; ga**47**)

After struggling in the Football League for a number of seasons, the Gulls were relegated to the Conference at the end of the 2006/07 season but prospered in their first season at this level but were ultimately defeated in the Play-Offs by local rivals Exeter City. However, a poor start to the team's second season in the Blue Square Premier saw the team win only one of its first seven League matches, leaving the Gulls languishing in 18th place. Form however picked up for Paul Buckle's team and the team was vying for a Play-Off place for much of the second half of the season, although it was not until the final League match of the season that a Play-Off berth was confirmed as a 2-1 victory over champions Burton Albion at Plainmoor ensured fourth place. In the Play-Offs United faced Histon. The first leg, at Plainmoor, resulted in a 2-0 victory for the home side and although the Cambridgeshire outfit was to achieve a 1-0 victory in the return match, the 2-1 aggregate win was enough to take United to Wembley to face another Cambridgeshire team – Cambridge United. A 2-0 victory was hard fought but ensured that League football returns to Torquay after a two-year gap. Away from the League, United had an impressive run in the FA Cup, defeating Championship side Blackpool in the Third Round 1-0 at Plainmoor before losing 1-0 to Coventry City. Teams promoted from the Conference have had varying fortunes over recent years; some have prospered – like rivals Exeter City – but others have struggled. Consolidation at this level will be the first priority for the team and this should be achievable.

Advance Tickets Tel No: 01803 328666
Fax: 01803 323976
Training Ground: Newton Abbot Racecourse, Newton Abbot, Devon TQ12 3AF
Brief History: Founded 1898 as Torquay United, amalgamated with Ellacombe in 1910 and name changed to Torquay Town. Amalgamated with Babbacombe in 1921 and name changed to Torquay United. Former Grounds: Teignmouth Road, Torquay Road, Cricketfield Road and Torquay Cricket Ground, moved to Plainmoor (Ellacombe's ground) in 1910. Relegated to the Conference in 2006/07 and promoted back to the Football League in 2008/09. Record attendance 21,908
(Total) Current Capacity: 6,283 (2,446 seated)
Visiting Supporters' Allocation: 1,100 (Sparkworld Away Stand) plus 200 seats (Main Stand)
Nearest Railway Station: Torquay (two miles)
Parking (Car): Street parking
Parking (Coach/Bus): Lymington Road coach station
Police Force and Tel No: Devon & Cornwall (08452 777444)
Disabled Visitors' Facilities:
Wheelchairs: Ellacombe End
Blind: No specific facility
Anticipated Development(s): The club has plans for the redevelopment of the Main Stand into a new 2,500-seat structure although there is no timescale for the work at present.

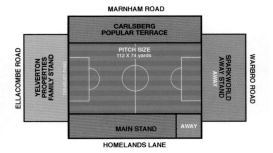

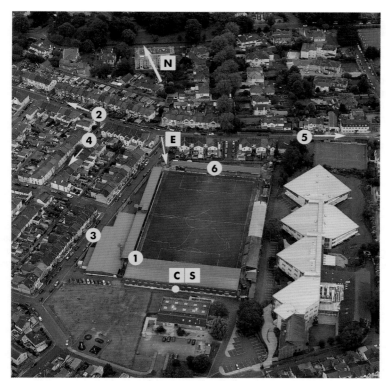

C Club Offices
S Club Shop
E Entrance(s) for visiting
   supporters

1 Warbro Road
2 B3202 Marychurch Road
3 Marnham Road
4 To Torquay BR station
   (two miles)
5 To A38
6 Sparkworld Away Stand

↑ North direction (approx)

◀ 700394
▼ 700393

tottenham hotspur

White Hart Lane, Bill Nicholson Way, 748 High Road, Tottenham, London N17 0AP

website: **WWW.TOTTENHAMHOTSPUR.COM**
e:mail: **CUSTOMER.CARE@TOTTENHAMHOTSPUR.COM**
tel no: **0844 499 5000**
colours: **WHITE SHIRTS, NAVY BLUE SHORTS**
nickname: **SPURS**
season 2009/10: **PREMIER LEAGUE**

Last Season: **8th** (p**38**; w**14**; d**9**; l**15**; gf**45**; ga**45**)

At one stage with Tottenham rooted in the bottom three it looked as though Juande Ramos's team was destined to make the drop to the second tier of English football for the first time since relegation at the end of the 1976/77 season. An appalling start to the season, which saw Spurs fail to win any of the opening eight League matches saw the team at the foot of the table with only two points on the board in the middle of October. Following a 2-0 defeat at Udinese in the UEFA Cup, the club acted and dismissed Ramos after only a year in charge. The club moved swiftly and appointed the Portsmouth boss, Harry Redknapp, to the managerial vacancy. Under Redknapp the team's performances improved although at Christmas the team was still in serious danger of relegation, sitting in 16th position but out of the drop zone only on goal difference. The club's first 20 League matches had brought a grand total of 20 points; the next 18, however, were to bring 31 and resulted in the team just missing out on a top seven place – and thus European football via the Europa League – via a slender margin. Redknapp has proved that he can achieve much in the Premier League and, in keeping Spurs in the Premier League and seeing the team rise up the table, he has laid the foundations for a more successful campaign in 2009/10. Whilst a top-four position may still be beyond the club's ability, it should certainly be in the mix for a Europa League place and, domestically, the team could well be a useful bet for either the Carling or FA Cup.

Ticket Line: 0844 844 0102
Fax: 020 8365 5005
Training Ground: Spurs Lodge, Luxborough Lane, Chigwell IG7 5AB
Brief History: Founded 1882 as 'Hotspur', changed name to Tottenham Hotspur in 1885. Former Grounds: Tottenham Marshes and Northumberland Park, moved to White Hart Lane in 1899. F.A. Cup winner 1901 (as a non-League club). Record attendance 75,038
(Total) Current Capacity: 36,257 (all seated)
Visiting Supporters' Allocation: 3,000 (in South and West Stands)
Nearest Railway Station: White Hart Lane plus Seven Sisters and Manor House (tube)
Parking (Car): Street parking (min ¼ mile from ground)
Parking (Coach/Bus): Northumberland Park coach park
Police Force and Tel No: Metropolitan (0208 801 3443)
Disabled Visitors' Facilities:
Wheelchairs: North and South Stands (by prior arrangement)
Blind: Commentary available
Anticipated Development(s): In late 2008 it was announced that Spurs intended to remain at White Hart Lane and redevelop the existing stadium into a 60,000-seat facility. In order to further this, the club had spent some £44 million acquiring properties around the existing site. Although no time-scale has as yet been announced, it seems unlikely that work will commence before 2011. The scheme, which includes a residential development and a museum, is estimated to cost some £400 million.

C Club Offices
S Club Shop
E Entrance(s) for visiting
   supporters

1 Park Lane
2 A1010 High Road
3 White Hart Lane BR station
4 Paxton Road
5 Worcester Avenue
6 West Stand
7 South Stand

↑ *North direction (approx)*

◁ 700261
▾ 700254

tranmere rovers

Prenton Park, Prenton Road West, Birkenhead, CH42 9PY

website: **WWW.TRANMEREROVERS.CO.UK**
e:mail: **INFO@TRANMEREROVERS.CO.UK**
tel no: **0871 221 2001**
colours: **WHITE SHIRTS, WHITE SHORTS**
nickname: **ROVERS**
season 2009/10: **LEAGUE ONE**

Last Season: **7th** (p**46**; w**21**; d**11**; l**14**; gf**62**; ga**49**)

So near and yet so far. For much of the final Saturday of the season, it looked as though Rovers would snatch the final Play-Off place from rivals Scunthorpe United during a tense match at Glanford Park. Needing to beat their hosts to leap frog them into the all-important sixth position, Rovers took the lead in the 39th minute courtesy of a goal by Craig Curran. As the second half progressed, the away fans' nerves must have got ever more strained, particularly after Rovers had Gareth Edds sent off. Reduced to 10 men Rovers conceded a free kick from which Scunthorpe's skipper Cliff Byrne scored an 88th-minute equaliser to take United through to the Play-Offs and consign Rovers to another season in League One. Hovering in or just outside the Play-Offs for most of the season, missing out will come as a bitter disappointment to the now departed Ronnie Moore and his team but the progress made on the field in 2008/09 will encourage a belief that, in 2009/10, the club can make more progress under new manager John Barnes and achieve the Play-Offs at the very least.

Advance Tickets Tel No: 0871 221 2001
Fax: 0151 609 0606
Training Ground: Raby Vale, Willaston Road, Clatterbridge CH63 4JG
Brief History: Founded 1884 as Belmont F.C., changed name to Tranmere Rovers in 1885 (not connected to earlier 'Tranmere Rovers'). Former grounds: Steele's Field and Ravenshaw's Field (also known as Old Prenton Park, ground of Tranmere Rugby Club), moved to (new) Prenton Park in 1911. Founder-members 3rd Division North (1921). Record attendance 24,424
(Total) Current Capacity: 16,587 (all seated)
Visiting Supporters' Allocation: 2,500 (all-seated) in Cow Shed Stand
Nearest Railway Station: Hamilton Square or Rock Ferry
Parking (Car): Car park at Ground
Parking (Coach/Bus): Car park at Ground
Other Clubs Sharing Ground: Liverpool Reserves
Police Force and Tel No: Merseyside (0151 709 6010)
Disabled Visitors' Facilities:
Wheelchairs: Main Stand
Blind: Commentary available

174

C Club Offices
S Club Shop
E Entrance(s) for visiting
   supporters

1 Car Park
2 Prenton Road West
3 Borough Road
4 M53 Junction 4 (B5151) –
   3 miles
5 Birkenhead (1 mile)
6 Cow Shed Stand
7 Kop Shed

↑ *North direction (approx)*

◄ 702200
▼ 702175

walsall

Banks's Stadium, Bescot Crescent, Walsall, West Midlands, WS1 4SA

website: **WWW.SADDLERS.CO.UK**
e:mail: **INFO@WALSALLFC.CO.UK**
tel no: **0871 221 0442**
colours: **RED SHIRTS, RED SHORTS**
nickname: **THE SADDLERS**
season2009/10: **LEAGUE ONE**

Last Season: **13th** (p**46**; w**17**; d**10**;l**19**; gf**61**; ga**66**)

Appointed manager in the close season, when Richard Money stood down following his failure to take the Saddlers to the League One Play-Offs, Jimmy Mullen was to last in the position only until early January when, following a run of only three wins in the previous eight League games, he departed. The club acted quickly in appointing ex-Wigan boss Chris Hutchings to the hot seat. In his previous managerial appointments, Hutchings had been appointed from within, succeeding Paul Jewell as manager at both Bradford City and Wigan and as caretaker manager following Jewell's departure from Derby County. When he was appointed, Hutchings inherited a team that was in 13th place; ironically, in the 22 games that he managed the club during the season – winning eight, drawing six and losing eight – the team was to finish in that self-same position. Outside of the League, the club was also to struggle in the Carling Cup, losing in the First Round to League Two Darlington at the Bescot Stadium 2-1. For 2009/10, Hutchings will be expected to make the Saddlers a more significant force in the hunt for the Play-Offs at the very least but a top-half finish is perhaps the best that the team might achieve.

Advance Tickets Tel No: 0870 442 0111
Fax: 01922 613202
Training Ground: The Pavilion, Broad Lane, Essington, Wolverhampton WV11 2RH
Brief History: Founded 1888 as Walsall Town Swifts (amalgamation of Walsall Town – founded 1884 – and Walsall Swifts – founded 1885), changed name to Walsall in 1895. Former Grounds: The Chuckery, West Bromwich Road (twice), Hilary Street (later named Fellows Park, twice), moved to Bescot Stadium in 1990. Founder-members Second Division (1892). Record attendance 11,049 (25,453 at Fellows Park)
(Total) Current Capacity: 11,300 (all seated)
Visiting Supporters' Allocation: 2,000 maximum in William Sharp Stand
Nearest Railway Station: Bescot
Parking (Car): Car park at Ground
Parking (Coach/Bus): Car park at Ground
Police Force and Tel No: West Midlands (01922 638111)
Disabled Visitors' Facilities:
Wheelchairs: Banks's Stand
Blind: No special facility
Anticipated Development(s): Planning permission was granted in the summer of 2004 for the redevelopment of the William Sharp Stand to add a further 2,300 seats, taking the away allocation up to 4,000 and the total ground capacity to 13,500. The project is to be funded via advertising directed towards the adjacent M6 but work has yet to commence.

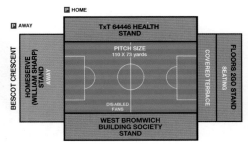

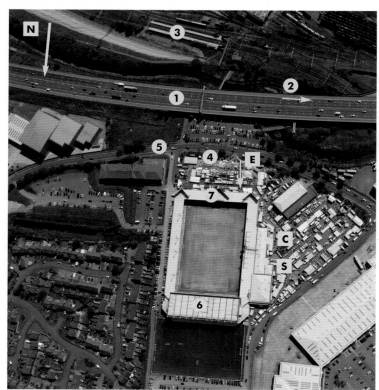

C Club Offices
S Club Shop
E Entrance(s) for visiting
supporters

1 Motorway M6
2 M6 Junction 9
3 Bescot BR Station
4 Car Parks
5 Bescot Crescent
6 Floors 2Go Stand
7 William Sharp (Homeserve)
Stand

↑ *North direction (approx)*

◄ 702570
▼ 702592

watford

Vicarage Road Stadium, Vicarage Road, Watford, WD18 0ER

website: **WWW.WATFORDFC.COM**
e:mail: **YOURVOICE@WATFORDFC.COM**
tel no: **0845 442 1881**
colours: **YELLOW SHIRTS, RED SHORTS**
nickname: **THE HORNETS**
season 2009/10: **CHAMPIONSHIP**

Last Season: **13th** (p**46**; w**16**; d**10**; l**20**; gf**68**; ga**72**)

Following a mediocre start to the season for Adrian Boothroyd's team, Watford deteriorated rapidly and after a 4-3 home defeat by Blackpool the manager was sacked in early November with the team in 21st place, only out of the relegation zone as a result of goal difference. Boothroyd had been at Vicarage Road for more than three years. The club appointed the ex-Chelsea coach Brendan Rodgers to his first managerial position later the same month. It took some time for the club's position to improve and relegation remained a serious threat until late in the season. Aided by five wins out of six League matches during February and March, the Hornets gradually climbed the Championship table. Outside the League, the club had some success in the Carling Cup, including a 1-0 victory over West Ham at home in the Third Round. Provided that the team can replicate its League form from the second half of the 2008/09 season for the new campaign the a good top half finish should certainly be achievable. However, the challenge will face a new manager, Malky Mackay, as Brendan Rodgers departed in June to take over at Reading.

Advance Tickets Tel No: 0845 442 1881

Fax: 01923 496001

Club Offices: Unit 3 Wolsey Business Park, Tolpits Lane, Watford WD18 9BL

Training Ground: University College London Sports Grounds, Bell Lane, London Colney, St Albans AL2 1BZ

Brief History: Founded 1898 as an amalgamation of West Herts (founded 1891) and Watford St. Mary's (founded early 1890s). Former Grounds: Wiggenhall Road (Watford St. Mary's) and West Herts Sports Ground, moved to Vicarage Road in 1922. Founder-members Third Division (1920). Record attendance 34,099

(Total) current Capacity: 19,900 (all seated)

Visiting Supporters' Allocation: 4,500 maximum in Vicarage Road (North) Stand

Nearest Railway Station: Watford High Street or Watford Junction

Parking (Car): Nearby multi-storey car park in town centre (10 mins walk)

Parking (Coach/Bus): Cardiff Road car park

Other Clubs Sharing Ground: Saracens RUFC

Police Force and Tel No: Hertfordshire (01923 472000)

Disabled Visitors' Facilities:

Wheelchairs: Corner East Stand and South Stand (special enclosure for approx. 24 wheelchairs), plus enclosure in North East Corner

Blind: Commentary available in the East Stand (20 seats, free of charge)

Anticipated Development(s): Although planning consent for the redevelopment of the East Stand was obtained in early 2008, work on the demolition of the original stand was delayed and the ground's capacity reduced to 17,500 for the 2008/09 season. In order to fund part of the work key-worker accommodation is being built around the stadium – as illustrated in the photographs – in conjunction with the Oracle housing association. Once all work is completed, including the construction of the new East Stand and the infill of the corners the ground's capacity will be 23,000. If work goes to schedule it should be completed by the start of the 2011/12 season.

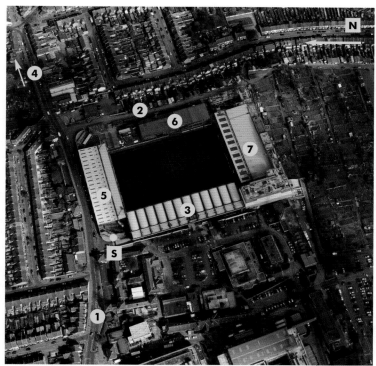

S Club Shop

1 Vicarage Road
2 Occupation Road
3 Rous Stand
4 Town Centre (½ mile) – Car
Parks, High Street BR Station
5 Vicarage Road Stand (away)
6 East Stand
7 Rookery End

↑ *North direction (approx)*

◀ 702385
▼ 702390

179

west bromwich albion

The Hawthorns, Halfords Lane, West Bromwich, West Midlands B71 4LF

website: **WWW.WBA.CO.UK**
e:mail: **ENQUIRIES@WBAFC.CO.UK**
tel no: **0871 271 1100**
colours: **NAVY BLUE AND WHITE STRIPED SHIRTS, WHITE SHORTS**
nickname: **THE BAGGIES**
season 2009/10: **CHAMPIONSHIP**

Last Season: **20th** (relegated) (p**38**; w**8**; d**8**; L**22**; gf**36**; ga**67**)

Under Tony Mowbray, West Brom had been promoted from the Championship at the end of the 2007/08 season and, as a promoted team, was always going to face the challenge of retaining top-flight status. A poor start to the season – three wins and three draws in the club's first 17 League matches – saw the Baggies rooted to the bottom of the table and the ill-fated last spot at Christmas belonged to the Baggies. Only one team had ever survived in the Premier League having been bottom at Christmas – West Brom in 2004/05 – and the question was, could the Baggies repeat the feat in 2008/09? Improved results seemed to suggest that it was possible but the gap was just too great and a 2-0 home defeat by Liverpool in the penultimate League match confirmed West Brom's relegation. It wasn't just in the League that the team struggled as defeats 3-1 after extra time away at Hartlepool in the First Round of the Carling Cup and 3-1 away at Burnley in the Fourth Round replay of the FA Cup demonstrated. The last time that the Baggies were relegated, it took two seasons for them to regain their Premier League status; as a relegated team the team will undoubtedly be one of the pre-season favourites for automatic promotion and the experience that the team has had in recent years should mean that the Play-Offs at the very least are a reasonable expectation. With Mowbray having departed to take over at Celtic, new boss Roberto di Matteo will face the challenge of restoring Premier League football to the Hawthorns.

Advance Tickets Tel No: 0871 271 9780
Fax: 0871 271 9861
Training Ground: West Bromwich Albion FC Development Centre, 430 Birmingham Road, Walsall WS5 3LQ
Brief History: Founded 1879. Former Grounds: Coopers Hill, Dartmouth Park, Four Acres, Stoney Lane, moved to the Hawthorns in 1900. Founder-members of Football League (1888). Record attendance 64,815
(Total) Current Capacity: 28,000 (all seated)
Visiting Supporters' Allocation: 3,000 in Smethwick End (can be increased to 5,200 if required)
Nearest Railway Station: The Hawthorns
Parking (Car): Halfords Lane and Rainbow Stand car parks
Parking (Coach/Bus): Rainbow Stand car park
Police Force and Tel No: West Midlands (0121 554 3414)
Disabled Visitors' Facilities:
Wheelchairs: Apollo 2000 and Smethwick Road End
Blind: Facility available
Anticipated Development(s): There is speculation that the club will seek to increase capacity to 30,000 by rebuilding the area between the Apollo and East stands, but nothing is confirmed.

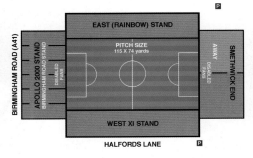

C Club Offices
S Club Shop
E Entrance(s) for visiting
supporters

1 A41 Birmingham Road
2 To M5 Junction 1
3 Birmingham Centre
(4 miles)
4 Halfords Lane
5 Main (West XI) Stand
6 Smethwick End
7 Rolfe Street, Smethwick BR
Station (1½ miles)
8 To The Hawthorns BR Station
9 East (Rainbow) Stand
10 Apollo 2000 Stand

⬆ *North direction (approx)*

◄ 701132
▼ 701130

west ham united

Boleyn Ground, Green Street, Upton Park, London, E13 9AZ

website: **WWW.WHUFC.COM**
e:mail: **YOURCOMMENTS@WESTHAMUNITED.CO.UK**
tel no: **020 8548 2748**
colours: **CLARET AND BLUE SHIRTS, WHITE SHORTS**
nickname: **THE HAMMERS**
season 2009/10: **PREMIER LEAGUE**

Last Season: **9th** (p**38**; w**14**; d**9**; l**15**; gf**42**; ga**45**)

Even before the start of the season Alan Curbishley's position as Hammers' boss seemed under threat, particularly given the way that certain key players such as Anton Ferdinand and George McCartney were transferred apparently against his wishes, and it came as little surprise that, despite a reasonably bright start to the season, he resigned in early September following a 4-1 defeat by Blackburn Rovers. The club moved quickly to appoint ex-Chelsea star Gianfranco Zola to the vacant manager's position. It took some time for Zola to find his managerial feet in the Premier League as the team won only three of his first 10 League matches in charge, results that left the Hammers in 13th place only two points above the drop zone half way through the season. By the start of March, however, the club's position was significantly improved, as the team stood in seventh place and chasing the final Europa League spot. Unfortunately, however, a late loss of form saw the team ultimately drift to a position mid-table. Away from the League, the club suffered a 1-0 defeat away at Championship outfit Watford in the Third Round of the Carling Cup. For 2009/10 Zola will further shape the team as he would like to see it in the close season and a further top-half position should be attainable with an outside possibility of a Europa League spot.

Advance Tickets Tel No: 0871 222 2700
Fax: 020 8548 2758
Training Ground: Chadwell Heath, Saville Road, Romford RM6 6DT
Brief History: Founded 1895 as Thames Ironworks, changed name to West Ham United in 1900. Former Grounds: Hermit Road, Browning Road, The Memorial Ground, moved to Boleyn Ground in 1904. Record attendance 42,322
(Total) Current Capacity: 35,303 (all seated)
Visiting Supporters' Allocation: 3,600 maximum
Nearest Railway Station: Barking BR, Upton Park (tube)
Parking (Car): Street parking
Parking (Coach/Bus): As directed by Police
Police Force and Tel No: Metropolitan (020 8593 8232)
Disabled Visitors' Facilities:
Wheelchairs: West Lower, Bobby Moore and Centenary Stands
Blind: Commentaries available
Anticipated Development(s): The idea that West Ham United might take over the 2012 Olympic Stadium was quashed in the spring of 2007. The club's new Icelandic owners have, however, decided to examine the possibility of relocation although nothing is confirmed at this stage.

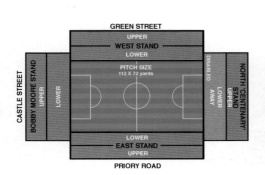

182

E Entrance(s) for visiting supporters

1 A124 Barking Road
2 Green Street
3 North Stand
4 Upton Park Tube Station (¼ mile)
5 Barking BR Station (1 mile)
6 Bobby Moore Stand
7 East Stand
8 West Stand

⬆ *North direction (approx)*

◀ 701322
▾ 701332

wigan athletic

DW Stadium, Robin Park Complex, Newtown, Wigan, Lancashire, WN5 0UZ

website: **WWW.WIGANLATICS.CO.UK**
e:mail: **S.HAYTON@JJBSTADIUM.CO.UK**
tel no: **01942 774000**
colours: **WHITE AND BLUE SHIRTS, BLUE SHORTS**
nickname: **THE LATICS**
season 2009/10: **PREMIER LEAGUE**

Last Season: **11th** (p**38**; w**12**; d**9**; l**17**; gf**34**; ga**45**)

Now reasonably well established in the Premier League, having survived four seasons in England's top division, Steve Bruce's Wigan Athletic had reached seventh place in the division by mid-January, having won nine out of the club's first 20 League matches. At this stage talk was more of a European place rather than the normal battle against relegation. However a run of only two wins in the club's last 18 League matches dragged the Latics down the table. It is perhaps significant that the decline in form took place after the January transfer window, when the club made a number of changes, most notably losing Wilson Palacios to Tottenham. With other players such as Antonio Valencia and Amr Zaki also likely to depart in the close season, Bruce's successor Roberto Martinez's challenge for 2009/10 will be to build a squad capable of keeping the team in the Premier League once more. Although ultimately the team finished mid-table, the club's form over the second half of the season will be a cause for concern for manager and fans alike and, given that the teams coming up from the Championship are arguably stronger than those promoted at the end of 2007/08, Wigan could again face a long hard winter to maintain Premier League status by May 2010.

Advance Tickets Tel No: 0871 663 3552
Fax: 01942 770477
Training Ground: Christopher Park, Wigan Lower Road, Standish Lower Ground, Wigan WN6 8LB
Brief History: Founded 1932. Springfield Park used by former Wigan Borough (Football League 1921-1931) but unrelated to current club. Elected to Football League in 1978 (the last club to be elected rather than promoted). Moved to DW (JJB) Stadium for start of 1999/2000 season. Record attendance at Springfield Park 27,500; at JJB Stadium 25,023
(Total) Current Capacity: 25,000 (all seated)
Visiting Supporters' Allocation: 5,400 (maximum) in North Stand (all-seated)
Nearest Railway Stations: Wigan Wallgate/Wigan North Western (both about 1.5 miles away)
Parking (Car): 2,500 spaces at the ground
Parking (Coach/Bus): As directed
Other Clubs Sharing Ground: Wigan Warriors RLFC
Police Force and Tel No: Greater Manchester (0161 872 5050)
Disabled Visitors' Facilities:
Wheelchairs: 100 spaces
Blind: No special facility although it is hoped to have a system in place shortly
Anticipated Development(s): None following completion of the ground.

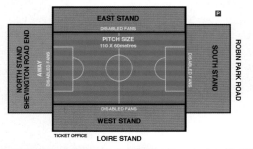

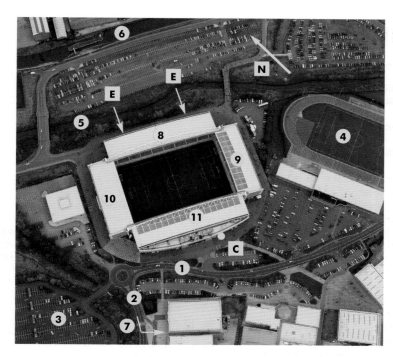

C Club Offices
E Entrance(s) for visiting
   supporters

1 Loire Drive
2 Anjoy Boulevard
3 Car Parks
4 Robin Park Arena
5 River Douglas
6 Leeds-Liverpool Canal
7 To A577/A49 and Wigan
   town centre plus Wigan
   (Wallgate) and Wigan
   (North Western) station
8 East Stand
9 South Stand
10 North Stand
11 West Stand

↑ *North direction (approx)*

◄ 701090
▼ 701097

wolverhampton wanderers

Molineux Ground, Waterloo Road, Wolverhampton, WV1 4QR

website: **WWW.WOLVES.CO.UK**
e:mail: **INFO@WOLVES.CO.UK**
tel no: **0871 222 2220**
colours: **GOLD SHIRTS, BLACK SHORTS**
nickname: **WOLVES**
season 2009/10: **PREMIER LEAGUE**

Last Season: **1st** (Promoted) (p**46**; w**27**; d**9**; l**10**; gf**80**; ga**52**)

A storming start to the season, with seven wins out of the club's first eight League matches, established Wolves as one of the teams to beat in the Championship and, by the end of November, following a run of seven straight wins, Mick McCarthy's team was top of the table by six points with a 12-point advantage already over third-placed Reading. However, come the New Year there was an alarming dip in form and a run of only one League win in 11 matches by the end of February saw Wolves still top, but the chasing teams closing up. The pressure from the fans was on the manager as all of the top teams in the Championship seemed determined not to achieve promotion. However, a return to form late in the season saw the team secure promotion following a 1-0 victory at Molyneux against QPR and the title the following match. McCarthy is an experienced manager and this should help the club survive for more than the one season that Wolves lasted in the Premier League the last time they reached English football's top table. However, the gulf between Championship and Premier League gets increasingly difficult to cross and Wolves will undoubtedly be a pre-season favourite for an immediate return to the Championship.

Advance Tickets Tel No: 0871 222 1877
Fax: 01902 687006
Training Ground: The Sir Jack Hayward Training Ground, Douglas Turner Way, Wolverhampton WV3 9BF
Brief History: Founded 1877 as St. Lukes, combined with Goldthorn Hill to become Wolverhampton Wanderers in 1884. Former Grounds: Old Windmill Field, John Harper's Field and Dudley Road, moved to Molineux in 1889. Founder-members Football League (1888). Record attendance 61,315
(Total) Current Capacity: 28,500 (all seated)
Visiting Supporters' Allocation: 3,200 in lower tier of Steve Bull Stand or 2,000 in Jack Harris Stand
Nearest Railway Station: Wolverhampton
Parking (Car): West Park and adjacent North Bank
Parking (Coach/Bus): As directed by Police
Police Force and Tel No: West Midlands (01902 649000)
Disabled Visitors' Facilities:
Wheelchairs: 104 places on two sides
Blind: Commentary (by prior arrangement)
Anticipated Developments: The club installed some 900 seats on a temporary stand – now removed – between the Billy Wright and Jack Harris stands. The club has plans to expand the capacity of Molineux to more than 40,000 by adding second tiers to the Stan Cullis and Jack Harris stands and completely rebuilding the Steve Bull Stand. There is, however, no confirmed timescale.

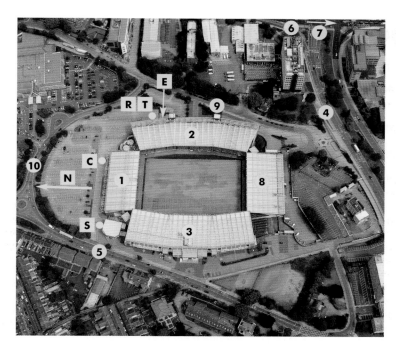

C **Club Offices**
S **Club Shop**
E **Entrance(s) for visiting supporters**
R **Refreshment bars for visiting supporters**
T **Toilets for visiting supporters**

1 **Stan Cullis Stand**
2 **Steve Bull Stand**
3 **Billy Wright Stand**
4 **Ring Road – St. Peters**
5 **Waterloo Road**
6 **A449 Stafford Street**
7 **BR Station (½ mile)**
8 **Jack Harris Stand**
9 **Molineux Street**
10 **Molineux Way**

⬆ *North direction (approx)*

◀ 700864
▼ 700855

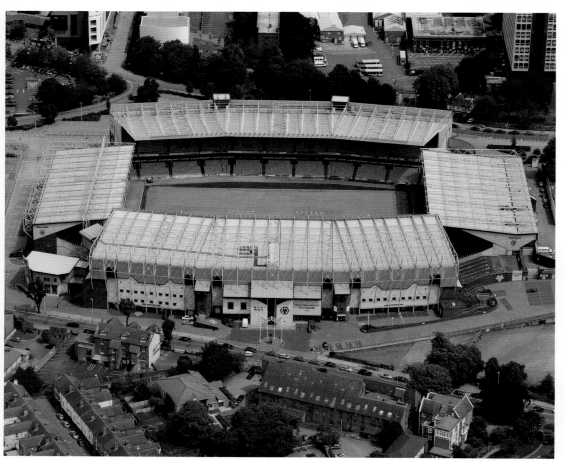

wycombe wanderers

Adams Park, Hillbottom Road, Sands, High Wycombe, Bucks HP12 4HJ

website: **WWW.WYCOMBEWANDERERS.CO.UK**
e:mail: **WWFC@WWFC.COM**
tel no: **01494 472 100**
colours: **SKY BLUE WITH NAVY BLUE QUARTERED SHIRTS, BLUE SHORTS**
nickname: **THE CHAIRBOYS**
season 2009/10: **LEAGUE ONE**

Last season: **3rd** (Promoted) (p**46**; w**20**; d**18**; l**8**; gf**54**; ga**33**)

Often the bridesmaid, rarely the bride, it has looked over recent seasons as though, despite early season form, that Wanderers invariably screw up their promotion campaign towards the end of the season and in 2008/09 the pattern seemed to be repeating itself. Unbeaten in the League until an away defeat at Aldershot in early December, Wycombe were by that stage already top of League Two with an eight-point advantage over fourth-placed Darlington. Ultimately, however, a dip in form and the onward march of teams such as Brentford, Exeter, Bury and Rochdale meant that the team's eventual fate was not to be determined until the final Saturday of the season. Three teams – Bury, Exeter and Wanderers – were all vying for the final two automatic promotion places. Exeter's victory at Rotherham guaranteed the Grecians the second automatic spot and Bury's 1-0 victory at home to Accrington put the pressure on Peter Taylor's side. A 2-1 home defeat to lowly Notts County, whilst probably causing considerable anxiety to the Adams Park faithful, was sufficient to see Wanderers scrape up to League One in third place over Bury, who were consigned to the Play-Offs on goal difference. Away from the League, Wanderers suffered the embarrassment of a 2-0 defeat away at non-League Eastwood at a time when Taylor's squad was still unbeaten in the League. Taylor is an astute operator at this level and his knowledge should give Wanderers the edge in potentially a hard struggle to survive in League One.

Advance Tickets Tel No: 01494 441118
Fax: 01494 527633
Training Ground: Marlow Road, Marlow, SL7 3DQ
Brief History: Founded 1884. Former Grounds: The Rye, Spring Meadows, Loakes Park, moved to Adams Park 1990. Promoted to Football League 1993. Record attendance 15,678 (Loakes Park); 10,000 (Adams Park)
(Total) Current Capacity: 10,000; (8,250 seated)
Visiting Supporters' Allocation: c2,000 in the Dreams (ex-Roger Vere) Stand
Nearest Railway Station: High Wycombe (2½ miles)
Parking (Car): At Ground and Street parking
Parking (Coach/Bus): At Ground
Other Clubs Sharing Ground: London Wasps RUFC
Police Force and Tel No: Thames Valley (01494 465888)
Disabled Visitors' Facilities:
Wheelchairs: Special shelter – Main Stand, Hillbottom Road end
Blind: Commentary available
Anticipated Development(s): The club is examining its options with a view to a possible relocation to a new 15,000-capacity stadium adjacent to Junction 4 of the M40 although nothing is confirmed at this stage.

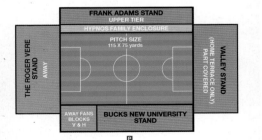

C Club Offices
S Club Shop
E Entrance(s) for visiting
   supporters

1 Car Park
2 Hillbottom Road
   (Industrial Estate)
3 M40 Junction 4
   (approx 2 miles)
4 Wycombe Town Centre
   (approx 2½ miles)
5 Woodlands Stand
6 Dreams Stand (away)
7 Syan Stand
8 Amersham & Wycombe
   College Stand

↑ North direction (approx)

◄ 701154
▾ 701160

yeovil town

Huish Park, Lufton Way, Yeovil, Somerset, BA22 8YF

website: **WWW.YTFC.NET**
e:mail: **JCOTTON@YTFC.NET**
tel no: **01935 423662**
colours: **GREEN SHIRTS, WHITE SHORTS**
nickname: **THE GLOVERS**
season 2009/10: **LEAGUE ONE**

Last season: **17th** (p**46**; w**12**; d**15**; l**19**; gf**41**; ga**66**)

After two-and-a-half years with Yeovil, Russell Slade departed as team manager in mid-February to be replaced by Terry Skiverton. Although Slade had guided the team to a position some eight points above the relegation zone on the back of four straight wins (equalling his best ever run with the club), his relationship with the board had become strained as a result of the limited funds available to him for the squad. Under Skiverton the club initially had a run of eight games without a win that dropped the team into the relegation zone and threatened the club's League One status. However, three wins and three draws in the final nine matches dragged the Glovers out of the mire and up to 17th place – one better than Slade had achieved at the end of the 2007/08 season. However, it's hard to escape the conclusion that Skiverton's team will face another uphill battle if they are to retain League One status in 2009/10.

Advance Tickets Tel No: 01935 423662
Fax: 01935 473956
Training Ground: No specific facility
Brief History: Founded as Yeovil Casuals in 1895 and merged with Petters United in 1920. Moved to old ground (Huish) in 1920 and relocated to Huish Park in 1990. Founder members of Alliance Premier League in 1979 but relegated in 1985. Returned to Premier League in 1988 but again relegated in 1996. Promoted to the now retitled Conference in 1997 and promoted to the Nationwide League in 2003. Record Attendance: (at Huish) 16,318 (at Huish Park) 9,348
(Total) Current Capacity: 9,665; (5,212 seated)
Visiting Supporters' Allocation: 1,700 on Copse Road Terrace (open) plus Limited seats in the Main Stand.
Nearest Railway Station: Yeovil Junction or Yeovil Pen Mill
Parking (Car): Car park near to stadium for 800 cars
Parking (Coach/Bus): As directed
Police Force and Tel No: Avon & Somerset (01935 415291)
Disabled Visitors' Facilities:
Wheelchairs: Up to 20 dedicated located in the Bartlett Stand
Blind: No special facility

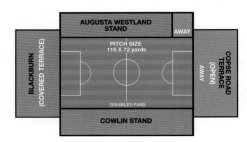

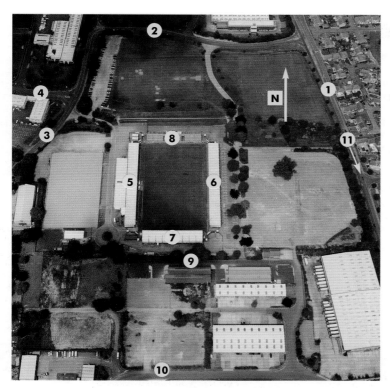

1 Western Avenue
2 Copse Road
3 Lufton Way
4 Artillery Road
5 Main (Yeovil College) Stand
6 Bartlett Stand
7 Westland Stand
8 Copse Road Terrace (away)
9 Memorial Road
10 Mead Avenue
11 To town centre (one mile)
  and stations (two to four
  miles)

⬆ North direction (approx)

◀ 700937
▼ 700947

millennium stadium

Millennium Stadium, Westgate Street, Cardiff, CF10 1JA

website: **WWW.MILLENNIUMSTADIUM.COM**
e:mail: **INFO@CARDIFF-STADIUM.CO.UK**
tel no: **0870 0138600**
Fax: **029 2082 2474**
Stadium Tours: **029 208 22228**

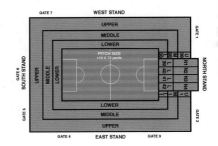

Brief History: The stadium, built upon the site of the much-loved and historic Cardiff Arms Park, was opened in 2000 and cost in excess of £100 million (a tiny sum in comparison with the current forecast spend of over £600 million on the redevelopment of Wembley). As the national stadium for Wales, the ground will be primarily used in sporting terms by Rugby Union, but was used by the FA to host major fixtures (such as FA Cup and Carling Cup finals) until 2007 when the new Wembley was completed.

(Total) Current Capacity: 72,500 (all seated)
Nearest Railway Station: Cardiff Central
Parking (Car): Street parking only.
Parking (Coach/Bus): As directed by the police
Police Force and Tel No: South Wales (029 2022 2111)
Disabled Visitors' Facilities:
Wheelchairs: c250 designated seats. The whole stadium has been designed for ease of disabled access with lifts, etc.
Blind: Commentary available.
Anticipated Development(s): None planned